An Introduction to Zimbabwean Law

An Introduction to Zimbabwean Law

LOVEMORE MADHUKU
BL (Hons), LLB (Zimbabwe), LLM, PhD (Cantab)

Lecturer in Law, Faculty of Law
University of Zimbabwe

Published by
Weaver Press, Box A1922,
Avondale, Harare
and
Friedrich-Ebert-Stiftung (FES)
Box 4720,
6 Ross Avenue
Belgravia, Harare

© FES & Lovemore Madhuku, 2010

Typeset by forzalibro designs
Cover by Danes Design, Harare
Printed by Sable Press, Harare

All rights reserved.
No part of the publication may be reproduced, stored in a retrieval system or transmitted in any form by any means – electronic, mechanical, photocopying, recording, or otherwise – without the express written permission of the copyright holders.

ISBN: 978-1-77922-098-1

About the author

Born on 20 July 1966 in Madhuku village, Lovemore Madhuku completed his primary and secondary education in Chipinge. He then completed his Bachelor of Law (Honours) degree in 1989 with a first-class pass at the University of Zimbabwe and went on to study for a post-graduate Bachelor of Laws (LLB) degree. Awarded a Beit Trust Fellowship to study law at Oxford University in the UK, he transferred after a term to study for the Master of Law (LLM) at the University of Cambridge on a Cambridge Commonwealth Trust Scholarship, completing with a first class in July 1994. He then returned to Zimbabwe for an 18-month break, during which time he joined the Friedrich Ebert-Stiftung, a German NGO, as a labour law consultant while at the same time teaching in the Law Faculty. In January 1996, he returned to the University of Cambridge to study for a PhD, which he successfully completed in December 1998. While still studying for his PhD, he accepted a permanent lectureship in the Law Faculty at the University of Zimbabwe. Since then, Madhuku has taught introduction to law, constitutional law, labour law, jurisprudence (legal theory), tax law, and banking law and has published extensively in these areas. He is currently Chairperson of the Department of Public Law in the Law Faculty.

Dr Madhuku is very active in civil society work. He is one of the founders of the National Constitutional Assembly (NCA) and has been its National Chairperson since July 2001. The NCA is advocating for a new, democratic and people-driven constitution in Zimbabwe.

He is married to Annamercy and they have three children, a daughter, Tendai, and two sons, Nyasha and Kuziyakwashe.

Contents

Acknowledgements	xiii
Foreword	xv

1 What is Law? — 1

- The concept of law: A definition — 1
- The relationship between law and morality — 3
- The relationship between law and justice — 4
- What is a legal system? — 6
  - *The purpose and function of law* — 6
    - To do justice — 7
    - To preserve peace and order — 7
    - To enforce morality — 8
    - To protect the interests of the ruling class — 10
- Two key elements of law: legal right and legal personality — 10
  - *Legal right* — 10
  - *Legal personality* — 11

2 Sources of Law — 13

- Legislation — 13
- Common law — 15
  - *A brief history of Roman Dutch law* — 18
  - *Advantages of precedent* — 24
- Custom — 25
  - *General custom* — 25
  - *African customary law* — 26
- Authoritative texts — 32
- Law reports — 33

3 Divisions of the Law — 36

- Criminal law versus civil law — 36
- Public law versus private law — 39
- Substantive law versus procedural law — 40

CONTENTS

National law versus international law — 40
General law versus customary law — 41
Common law versus civil law — 41
Law (common law) versus equity — 41

4 The Law-Making Process — 43

Introduction: State organs and their powers — 43
The legislature (the law-makers) — 44
The executive — 46
The judiciary — 47
Other key organs — 48
The Attorney General — 48
The Comptroller and Auditor-General — 49
The Public Protector — 49
The process of law-making in Parliament — 49
Pre-bill stage — 50
Types of bills — 51
Gazetting of bills — 51
Passage of bills in Parliament — 52
The effect of Parliament's failure to follow specified procedures — 55
Delegated legislation — 57

5 The Structure of the Courts — 61

The division between criminal courts and civil courts — 61
Criminal courts — 61
Magistrates Courts — 62
Composition — 62
Jurisdiction — 63
The High Court — 64
Composition — 64
Jurisdiction — 66
The Supreme Court — 67
Composition — 67
Jurisdiction — 67
Courts-martial — 68
Police board of officers — 68
Prison courts — 68

CONTENTS

Children's Courts	68
Parliament sitting as a court over breach of parliamentary privileges	69
Ordinary civil courts	70
Magistrates Courts	70
Jurisdiction	70
Composition	71
The High Court	71
Composition	71
Jurisdiction	71
The Supreme Court	72
Composition	72
Jurisdiction	72
Specialist courts	73
Advantages of specialist courts	73
Disadvantages of specialist courts	74
Examples of specialist courts	74
The Labour Court	74
The Administrative Court	76
The Administrative Court as the Water Court	76
Special court for income tax appeals	78
Local courts on customary law	79
Small Claims Court	80

6 The Legal Profession in Zimbabwe — 84

Introduction: The legal profession	84
A divided or fused profession?	84
The nature of the fused profession in Zimbabwe	86
Admission as a legal practitioner	87
Practical legal training after registration	89
Discipline for professional misconduct	89
The Law Society of Zimbabwe	90
The Council for Legal Education	91
Judges	91
Who appoints judges?	92
Qualifications for appointment as judges	94
Compulsory retirement versus executive discretion to extend the term of office of a judge	95
The removal of judges from office	96

CONTENTS

    Other features on the independence of judiciary   103
        Provision on judicial independence   103
        Vesting judiciary functions exclusively in the judiciary   104

7 An Outline of Court Procedures   107

    Civil procedures   107
        Adversarial versus inquisitorial procedure   107
        Civil trial procedure versus application procedure   108

    Civil trial procedure   108
        Letter of Demand   108
        Issue of Summons   108
        Appearance to defend   109
        Request for further particulars   109
        Defendant's plea   109
        Request for further particulars   109
        Replication   110
        Close of pleadings   110
        Discovery   110
        Pre-trial conference   110
        Trial date   110
        The trial   110
        Judgment   111
        Enforcement of judgment   111
            Execution of property   111
            Garnishee order   111
            Civil imprisonment   111

    Contempt of court   112

    Appeals and reviews   113
        Application procedure   114

    Criminal procedure   115
        General   115
        Securing presence of the accused   116
        Bail   117
        The trial process   117

    Stages of the trial process   118
        The accused's entering of plea   118
        Outline of the State's case   119
        Outline of the defence   119
        Evidence-in-chief   119

Cross-examination	119
Re-examination	120
Closing of the State case	120
Application for discharge of the accused at the close of state case (optional)	120
Defence case	120
Close of the defence case	121
Addresses by both sides	121
Verdict	121
Addresses on sentence: mitigation/aggravation	121
Sentencing	122
Caution or reprimand	122
Fines	122
Recognisances	123
Community service	123
Imprisonment	123
Corporal punishment	124
Sentencing to death	124

8 Legal Aid — 127

Introduction	127
The old system of legal aid	128
Civil court legal aid	128
Criminal court legal aid	128
The new system of legal aid	130
Evaluation of the Legal Aid Scheme in terms of the Act	133
Contingency fee arrangements	134
Legal aid by non-governmental organisations	135
The English legal aid system	136
Legal aid in South Africa	140

9 Statutory Interpretation — 144

Introduction	144
The objective of interpretation	144
Rules of statutory interpretation	145
The Literal Rule	145
Statement of the rule	145
Application of the Literal Rule	146

- *The Golden Rule* — 150
  - Statement of the rule — 150
  - Application of the Golden Rule — 150
- *The Mischief Rule* — 151
  - Application of the Mischief Rule — 152
  - The special place of a casus omissus — 152
- *Maxims of statutory interpretation* — 153
  - 'Ejusdem generis' — 154
  - 'Noscitur a sociis' — 156
  - 'The rule of rank' — 156
  - 'Expression unius est exclusio alterius' — 157
  - 'Contemporanea expositio' — 158
  - 'Reddendo singula singulis' — 158
  - 'Cessante ratione legis, cessat ipsa lex' — 159
- Presumptions of statutory interpretation — 160
  - *Introduction: What are presumptions?* — 160
  - *Specific presumptions* — 162
    - The presumption against the alteration of the common law more than is necessary — 162
    - The presumption that the legislature does not intend that which is harsh, unjust or unreasonable — 163
    - The presumption of constitutionality — 164
    - The presumption against retrospectivity — 166
    - The presumption in favour of the principles of natural justice — 166
    - The presumption against interpreting a statute so as to oust or restrict the jurisdiction of the Superior Courts — 168
- Aids to statutory interpretation — 168
  - *The Interpretation Act (Chapter 1:01)* — 168
  - *Interpretation of sections of a statute* — 170
    - Preamble — 170
    - The long title — 172
    - The short title — 173
    - Headings and marginal notes — 173
    - Punctuation — 174
    - Schedules — 174
  - *External aids* — 174
    - Historical background or surrounding circumstances — 174
    - Parliamentary history, including parliamentary debates — 175
    - Statutes *in pari materia* — 176
    - Treaties and International Conventions — 177
- Some Latin words and expressions — 183

Acknowledgements

This book is a compilation of my lecture notes for 'Introduction to Law', a course which is one of the main foundations of the LLB degree of the Faculty of Law, University of Zimbabwe. I have taught this first-year course to students in the Faculty of Law for the last fourteen years. I have also been a consultant for the Friedrich-Ebert-Stiftung (FES) since 1995, where I have been involved in a paralegal training programme for trade unionists who are members of the Zimbabwe Congress of Trade Unions (ZCTU). The ZCTU paralegal programme has a subject called 'Introduction to Law' and is deliberately based on the framework used for first-year law students at the University of Zimbabwe.

There are those who deserve special mention for making the publication of this book a success. I would like to register my indebtedness to the Friedrich-Ebert-Stiftung for funding the publication of this book. The gestation period for this book was somewhat lengthy. I very much appreciate the open hand shown by successive FES Directors: Rudolf Traub-Merz, Felix Schmidt, Sven Schwersensky, Gerd Botterweck and Kathrin Meissner. Local FES staff Florence and Tendayi were equally supportive.

All my law students have been a tremendous source of inspiration. To them I owe the insights that have enabled me to determine what to include in this book. My colleagues in the Faculty of Law have also assisted me in many ways: Ellen Sithole and Joel Zowa, with materials on the procedural law aspects of the book; Geoff Feltoe and Emmanuel Magade, by encouraging me to complete this book; and Munyaradzi Gwisai, by pre-testing some of the ideas in the book.

Outside the academic world, I have a solid support group that deserves my appreciation. With the formation of the National Constitutional Assembly (NCA) in 1997, and my active involvement in it, my academic work underwent a metamorphosis of some sort. Activism began to take up a greater portion of my time. This fusion between activism and academic work had interesting results. For example, just as the police found it easier to preempt NCA protests by arresting me outside university lecture rooms, many students came to find it more convenient to submit their assignments and draft dissertations at the NCA Head Office at Bumbiro House. Thus, both the University and the NCA felt the effects of the two worlds that I kept together. In this respect, I would like to thank both activists and the Secretariat of the NCA for supporting my academic work.

At the technical level, Abgail Mawonya, our secretary at the University's Public Law Department, played a very pivotal role. She typed up lecture notes, kept them for the next group of students and when the time came for converting lecture notes into chapters of this book, she provided excellent assistance. She was assisted by Fungai Chinyani (FES), who also typed and kept a significant portion of my lecture materials. Fungai Mufudzi (NCA) also found herself involved in typing and keeping some of the materials that were developed while I was at the NCA.

I thank Weaver Press, its director, Irene Staunton, and her team for an excellent editing job and, above all, for their patience – they waited three years for the final version of the manuscript!

The last and most important appreciation is reserved for my family. My wife, Annamercy, and my own children (Tendai, Nyasha and Kuziyakwashe) have that unique contribution of being an unshakeable base from which all becomes possible. I give every word of appreciation to my parents and my mother-in-law, my brothers and brothers-in-law, sisters and sisters-in-law, Tadiwanashe, and all our family in its extended sense, for their unconditional support. Finally, I must mention *mainini* Bongi, for all the work she did for this book to be published. She exceeded the bounds of duty and made this her personal project.

Foreword

The Friedrich-Ebert-Stiftung (FES) is a German political foundation that was established in 1925. The oldest political foundation in Germany, its backbone is the promotion of the ideas and values of social democracy across the world. It carries out its mission through its programmes of civic education, research, the strengthening of democratic institutions and support of programmes that promote social justice.

The FES has worked in Zimbabwe since the country's independence in 1980. Its main work has been in cooperating with trade unions, encouraging initiatives in democratic reform and promoting public debate on social, economic and political issues.

The foundation's support for the publication of this book emanates from its paralegal training programme with the trade unions under the auspices of the Zimbabwe Congress of Trade Unions. The book started as an *Introduction to Law for Trade Unionists*. From this, its author, Dr Lovemore Madhuku, who is both a University lecturer and an FES consultant, was able to produce a book suitable for both paralegal training and university studies. The FES sees this book as a great asset in legal education in Zimbabwe and is therefore proud to support its publication.

It is hoped that this book will play a role in the development of Zimbabwe by being useful to law students, lawyers, paralegal trainees and the general public.

Kathrin Meissner
Resident Director, FES Zimbabwe
January, 2010

1

What is Law?

The concept of law: A definition

Law refers to rules and regulations that govern human conduct or other societal relations and are enforceable by the state. It is the quality of enforceability by the state that distinguishes law from other rules. There are, of course, other rules that govern human conduct such as moral rules, religious directives and organizational rules. These other rules may even be more effective in ensuring compliance with a particular type of conduct. They may even be more acceptable. However, it is not the effectiveness of rules or their goodness/badness that determines the legal quality. It is, in fact, the sole factor of enforceability by the state that determines whether a rule is law or not. It has been said:

> Although the notion of a system of rules probably corresponds closely to most people's idea of law, we can soon see that this is not sufficient by itself to be an accurate or adequate account of law, because there are, in any social group, various systems of rules apart from law. How do we distinguish, for example, between a legal rule and a moral rule? In our society, though we consider it immoral to tell lies, it is not generally against the law to do so. Of course, some moral rules are also embodied in the law, such as the legal rule prohibiting murder. Again, how do we distinguish between a legal rule and a rule of custom or etiquette?[1]

What distinguishes a legal rule from any other rule is that a legal rule is one that is recognized as law and is enforceable by the state.

In order to understand the nature of law, reference must be made to the two main theories of law, namely, the *natural law theory* and the *positivist theory*. According to the theory of natural law, law cannot be separated from the precepts of morality, justice or fairness. It says that a set of moral principles exists that have validity and authority independent of any human authority. These moral principles, which have a higher status than any human-made rules, constitute what is termed 'natural law'. Any human-made law that contradicts 'natural law' is invalid. In other words, a law that is unfair or immoral, in the sense that it is contrary to natural law, is no law at all. The Latin maxim *'lex iniusta non est lex'* (an unjust law is no law at all) aptly underscores the main idea of natural law.

By contrast, the positivist theory says law is law, regardless of its moral content and regardless of whether it is just or unjust. The positivist theory distinguishes law *as it is* from law *as it ought to be*. There is, therefore, such a thing as an unjust law, a bad law, an immoral law, and so on. What law is, is one thing, but its goodness or badness is another.

The positivist theory of law is the prevailing doctrine in the definition of law. It is applied by almost every legal system in ascertaining what the law is in any given situation. In other words, when answering the question – what does the law say in this situation? – one does not attempt to establish what is just or morally acceptable in the given situation. Instead, one must simply ascertain the applicable rule of law, regardless of whether it is seemingly just or unjust, fair or unfair, moral or immoral. What matters is whether or not it is a rule recognized and enforceable by the state. If it is enforceable by the state, it is law.

South African lawyers H.R. Hahlo and Ellison Kahn neatly captured the nature of law in the following passage:

> [T]he next question we have to answer is: what distinguishes the law of the lawyer ... from other practical laws, such as moral law, the laws of etiquette or the laws of cricket? The answer is that law in the strict sense is the only body of rules governing human conduct that is recognized as binding by the state and, if necessary, enforced. This does not mean that there are no sanctions as far as other practical laws are concerned. There is the conscience of the individual, the pressure of public opinion, social approval or disapproval. But only law in the strict sense is enforced by the courts of law or some other organ of the state.[2]

Given this definition of law, the key question that arises is: How do we determine that a particular rule is recognized and enforceable by the state? The answer is that for a rule to be recognized and enforceable by the state, and therefore for it to be called *law*, it must emanate from a recognized source. There are four sources of law, namely, legislation (statutes), common law, custom and authoritative texts. A rule is a rule of law if – and only if – it can be derived from one of these four sources. These are discussed in chapter two.

The definition of law given above raises critical issues about the relationship between law and morality and between law and justice. It is important to discuss these relationships in order to get a fuller understanding of the concept of law.

The relationship between law & morality

Law is law, regardless of its moral content. However, most legal rules are derived from morality. This means that in such instances, the law is used to enforce morality. Law-makers seeking to enact new laws to regulate human conduct usually convert into law their deeply held moral convictions. Morality is the bedrock of law but it is not law. Take, for example, the following rule: 'Thou shall not kill'. This is a rule of morality. If the state decides to recognize and enforce it, it also becomes a legal rule. If the state decides not to convert it into law, it remains a moral rule only.

A moral rule is converted into law in three main ways. First, a moral rule that is considered by a given society as so important as to require legal backing is converted into law by the simple device of enacting a piece of legislation incorporating that moral rule. Once enacted, the piece of legislation becomes the source of the legal rule, but this does not take away the fact that its real source is morality. For example, most people in Zimbabwe would regard it as immoral for any person to engage in any form of sexual activity with an animal. This moral perception has been converted into law through the creation of the crime of bestiality, which is provided for in Section 74 of the Criminal Law (Codification and Reform) Act (Chapter 9:23) as follows:

> Any person who knowingly commits any sexual act with an animal or bird shall be guilty of bestiality and liable to a fine up to or exceeding level fourteen or imprisonment for a period not exceeding one year or both.

The second way in which a moral rule may be converted into law is in the so-called 'grey areas' of the law, i.e., where the law is unclear and the courts resort to moral principles in interpreting the law. An interpretation made by a court is legally binding for the purposes of the issue at stake

WHAT IS LAW?

and, as shall be seen later under the common law system, it becomes, in appropriate cases, part of the law. In this way, moral principles are converted into law via the device of being utilized in the interpretation of unclear legal provisions. A prominent example worth noting includes the English case of *Corbett v Corbett*, where the court was called upon to determine whether or not a man and a person who had undergone a sex change to 'become' a woman could enter into a valid marriage at law.[3] The court held that the purported 'marriage' was invalid. It resorted to what was then regarded as morally correct, namely, that marriage had to be between a biological man and a biological woman and that a sex change could not *make* a man a woman. This is what the judge said:

> Since marriage is essentially a relationship between a man and a woman, the validity of the marriage in this case depends in my judgment, upon whether the respondent is or is not a woman .... Having regard to the essentially heterosexual character of the relationship which is called marriage, the criteria must in my judgment, be biological, for even the most extreme degree of transsexualism in a male or the most severe hormonal imbalance which can exist in a person with male chromosomes, male gonads and male genitalia cannot reproduce a person who is naturally capable of performing the essential role of a woman in marriage.[4]

Another useful example is the famous American case of *Riggs v Palmer*.[5] In this instance, the court was asked to decide whether or not a grandson named in the will of his grandfather could be allowed to inherit, given that he had murdered his grandfather in order to gain his inheritance. In general, a person named as heir under a will is entitled to inherit. The court, however, found it immoral to allow a murderer to inherit. It invoked the moral principle that 'no one shall be permitted to profit by his own fraud, or to take advantage of his own wrong, or to found any claim upon his own iniquity or to acquire property by his own crime' and denied the murderer his inheritance.

The third way in which a moral rule may be converted into law is through custom. Some moral rules, by sheer force of their wide acceptance and observance, may graduate into a binding custom. As is explained later, custom is a source of law.

The relationship between law & justice

Law is law, regardless of whether it is just or unjust. Most legal rules are designed to achieve the ends of justice. As with morality, law-makers seeking to enact laws to regulate human conduct usually justify their enactment on the basis of justice. As Johannes Voet puts it, 'The law ought to be just and reasonable, both in regard to the subject matter, directing what is honourable, forbidding what is base and as to its form, preserving equality and binding the citizens equally'.[6] Similarly, the fact that a rule is law does not necessarily mean that it is just. However, justice is an external standard against which law may be measured and an 'unjust' law is as much law as a 'just' law.

The 'difficulty' with justice is that it is almost impossible to state exactly what it is. It is submitted that justice is fairness. That fairness lies at the core of justice is reflected in almost all attempts to define justice. The *Oxford English Reference Dictionary* (2003) defines 'just' as 'acting or done in accordance with what is morally right or fair' and 'justice' as 'just conduct, fairness'. *Blacks Law Dictionary* (2004) states that justice is 'the fair and proper administration of laws'.

It is important to understand the two senses in which the word 'justice' may be used. These two senses are clearly captured by Hilaire McCoubrey and Nigel D. White:

> 'Justice' is a commonly encountered term of legal rhetoric and to deal 'justly' is held out as a fundamental aspiration of a legal system. At the same time, the intention which this rhetoric supposedly reflects is often less than clear. In practice, a distinction is drawn between 'justice according to the law' and 'justice' as an ideal form of dealing. In the former case, little more is meant than the proper operation of a given system, albeit subject to some very basic expectations of due process. In the latter case, an external standard is being advanced by reference to which the operation of the legal system may be evaluated.[7]

In the first sense of justice, i.e., 'according to law', it is served whenever the law is faithfully executed, whatever the content. In the second sense of justice as an 'ideal form of dealing', justice relates to the substance of the law and is an external yardstick. It is this sense of justice that is discussed here as 'fairness'. It is this same sense of justice with which the law may or may not comply. Both senses of justice are discussed in the following:

> If a rule stipulates that all motorists exceeding a speed limit shall be fined, but those exacting fines take no [or insufficient] steps to find out whether people have fulfilled the conditions of the rule, then [justice according to law] is violated .... If, during a period of political turbulence, a revolutionary 'court' selects victims for execution on an ad hoc basis, without announcing any universal criteria for distinguishing those subject to punishment from those not, it violates [justice according to law] .... If a revolutionary court announces that all those who voted for an ousted regime are to be shot, and takes diligent

steps in each case to find out whether or not a person had so voted, it meets the requirements of [justice according to law] but it still might be claimed to be violating [justice as an ideal form of dealing].[8]

It should be clear, therefore, that whenever justice is regarded as an external measure of the law, law may be considered just or unjust. Accordingly, one may follow the law to the letter, but the outcome may still be unjust because the law itself is unjust. Given that law is law regardless of its fairness, a court of law is obliged to enforce the law *as it is*, regardless of that court's perception of justice. This point was admirably underscored by Ebrahim JA in his dissenting judgment in *Minister of Lands & Ors v Commercial Farmers Union*:

> During argument, the view was expressed that justice was on the applicants' side, but the law was on the respondent's side. Admittedly law and justice do not always coincide. Examples of oppressive and unjust laws can be found in many countries. But this does not mean that the courts, which are sworn to uphold the law can ever allow their personal, subjective view of what constitutes justice to override the clear provisions of the law.
>
> It is not the function of the courts to support the government of the day, or the would-be government of tomorrow. It is not their function to support the state against the individual or the individual against the state. The courts' duty is to the law and to the law alone. Judges, as individuals, have their own political, legal and social views and opinions. But it is the sworn duty of every judge to apply the law, whatever he or she may think of the law. If a law is patently unjust, the courts can seek to better matters as far as possible, within the law, but they may never subvert the law. The remedy for an unjust law lies, not with the courts, but with the legislature.[9]

What is a legal system?

A legal system is the sum total of the law of a given society, and includes the way(s) it is made, how it is enforced and the institutions involved in its making and enforcement.

The purpose & function of law

The traditional approach to the role and function of law is that it has two main purposes, namely, (i) to do justice, and (ii) to preserve peace and order. Although legal theories are divided on the proper role of law, this traditional approach is a useful starting point to understanding the various purposes and functions of law. Four of these are discussed below.

To do justice

Law must serve the ends of justice, and this function is accepted by all legal systems. It has already been said that the 'problem' with justice is that it is difficult to say what justice is. Moreover, what is just for one person may not be just for another. Accordingly, to say that law must serve the ends of justice is to promote the view of justice shared by those whose perceptions dominate a given society. It has been aptly said that:

> The substance of justice is as much, if more, a question of political philosophy as of jurisprudence. It is ultimately a question of perceptions of the relations of human beings in society.[10]

Whatever the prevalent notion of justice, what is undeniable is that law ought to serve the ends of justice. Given that different persons or groups of persons have different conceptions of justice, it is legitimate for those who view existing law as unjust to seek to achieve what they perceive as a just law through political debate or, if that fails, by attaining political power by democratic means and using that power to enact what they believe to be just law.

To preserve peace & order

This purpose is regarded by Hahlo and Kahn as the 'foremost purpose of law'. They express it as follows:

> The first and foremost purpose of law is to maintain peace and order in the community. Man must live in society if he is to achieve his full development. Society, however, cannot exist without law, for without rules of conduct there cannot be order, and without order there cannot be peace and progress.[11]

While the preservation of peace and order is an important function of law, it cannot truly be described as the 'first and foremost purpose'. To describe it as such may seem to suggest that peace and order can be pursued to the exclusion of everything else. This is not so. The preservation of peace and order must be sought with due regard to justice and respect for fundamental human rights. Many autocratic regimes defend their resort to draconian laws that infringe basic human rights by appealing to the 'overriding need to preserve peace and order'. It is unacceptable for law to be justified solely by reference to 'peace and order'. Indeed, in the majority of cases, law must seek to attain peace and order by conforming to acceptable notions of justice. A just law is more likely to be observed than an unjust one. An unjust law invites disobedience and may ultimately lead to disorder.

To enforce morality

This purpose of the law is separate from that of promoting justice in one respect: justice is merely one component of morality. There are other components of morality that the concept of justice does not embrace and it is these other components that are covered here. Professor Herbert Hart describes the relationship between justice and morality as follows:

> Justice constitutes one segment of morality primarily concerned not with individual conduct but with the ways in which *classes* of individuals are treated. It is this which gives justice its special relevance in the criticism of law and of other public or social institutions. It is the most public and the most legal of the virtues. But principles of justice do not exhaust the idea of morality, and not all criticism of law made on moral grounds is made in the name of justice. Laws may be condemned as morally bad simply because they require men to do particular actions which morality forbids individuals to do, or because they require men to abstain from doing those which are morally obligatory.
>
> It is therefore necessary to characterize, in general terms, those principles, rules, and standards relating to the conduct of individuals which belong to morality and make conduct morally obligatory. Two related difficulties confront us here. The first is that the word 'morality' and all other associated or nearly synonymous terms like 'ethics' have their own considerable area of vagueness or 'open texture'. There are certain forms of principle or rule which some would rank as moral and which others would not. Secondly, even where there is agreement on this point and certain rules or principles are accepted as indisputably belonging to morality, there may still be great philosophical disagreement as to their *status* or relation to the rest of human knowledge and experience.[12]

Morality that is not covered by the concept of justice may be enforced by law. The main difficulty remains that alluded to in the above passage, that is, establishing the nature of morality. Professor Lon Fuller has warned us against the often-encountered assumption that everyone knows what morality entails. He has the following instructive passage:

> [There is] a dissatisfaction with the existing literature concerning the relation between law and morality. This literature seems to me to be deficient in two important respects. The first of these relates to a failure to clarify the meaning of morality itself. Definitions of law we have in almost unwanted abundance. But when law is compared with morality, it seems to be assumed that everyone knows what the second term of the comparison embraces.[13]

Notwithstanding this useful observation, the assumption that everyone has some idea of what morality embraces is not misplaced. The scope of this book proceeds from that assumption. The issue here is whether or not law should be used to enforce morality, whatever the nature of morality.

The dominant view is that law has a legitimate purpose to enforce morality. Differences arise as to the extent of the use of law in this regard, it being clear that not every moral rule needs to be enforced by law. Some have argued for a very minimal role for law, while others have gone for the maximum possible under the legal system.

Those who have argued for a minimum role have been inspired, among others, by the ubiquitous John Stuart Mill. In his 1859 essay on liberty, he wrote that:

> The object of this Essay is to assert one very simple principle, as entitled to govern absolutely the dealings of society with the individual in the way of compulsion and control, whether the means used be physical force in the form of legal penalties, or the moral coercion of public opinion. That principle is, that the sole end for which mankind are warranted, individually or collectively, in interfering with the liberty or action of any of their number, is self-protection. That the only purpose for which power can be rightfully exercised over any member of a civilized community, against his will, is to prevent harm to others. His own good, either physical or moral, is not a sufficient warrant.[14]

A proper interpretation of the above views in relation to morality is this: law must only enforce morality to prevent harm to others, but where an immoral act harms no one but oneself, the law must not be involved. This approach found a practical application in the United Kingdom in 1957 over the issue of homosexuality. The government had appointed a committee under the chairmanship of Sir John Wolfenden to make recommendations on how prostitution and homosexuality should be treated by criminal law. The committee published its report in 1957 and made two recommendations, namely, that (i) while prostitution itself should not be punishable as it harms no one apart from the participants, soliciting on the streets by prostitutes should be punished as it harmed others; and (ii) homosexual acts between consenting adults in private should no longer be a criminal offence as this behaviour harmed no one except the participants. These recommendations were eventually enacted into law and represent the minimal approach to the use of law to enforce morality.

The dominant view – that it is a legitimate purpose of law to enforce morality – is supported by most legal systems and has been defended by Lord Devlin, a prominent British jurist. According to Devlin, every society has a right to punish any kind of act that is grossly immoral. The test is not whether or not the act in question harms any person. The test of what is grossly immoral is that of 'the right-minded man' ('the man in the jury-box') and his/her socially moral opinion. According to him, the reason for using law to enforce morality is to achieve 'social cohesion' rather than endorse its degradation.

To protect the interests of the ruling class

According to the Marxist theory of law, law has one main purpose: to protect and promote the interests of the ruling class. The Marxist theory was developed by Karl Marx (1818–83) and Friedrich Engels (1820–95). It is built on the principles of dialectical materialism that view all things and phenomena in nature as interconnected and conditioned by each other. More fundamentally, the theory is founded on the thesis that it is the material conditions of society that determine everything else in human institutions. These material conditions find expression in the economic structure of society. Marx distinguished between the economic structure of society (which he called the 'base') and the superstructure, which was determined by the base. Law is a component of the superstructure and is controlled by the base (the economic structure). As the ruling class owns the means of economic production, it controls the base and uses the law to protect its interests.

The ruling class suppresses other classes in order to remain in control of the economic means of production. Under capitalism, the ruling class suppresses and exploits the working class. In this regard, it deploys the law as an instrument of suppression and exploitation.

There is a great deal of substance in the Marxist conception of law. However, the theory exaggerates the extent to which law is an instrument of ruling class interests. While law is, in many respects, an instrument of class rule, it is also, in other respects, a phenomenon that has life outside the realm of class struggle.

Two key elements of law: legal right & legal personality

With the understanding of law discussed in this opening chapter, it is important to explain two key elements: *legal right* and *legal personality*.

Legal right

A legal right may be defined as 'an interest conferred by and protected by the law, entitling one person to claim that another person or persons either give him/her/it something, or do an act for him/her/it or refrain from doing an act'.[15]

There are, of course, other rights such as moral rights, which entitle persons to claim from others that they do or not do certain acts. But a right is a *legal right* if – and only if – it is conferred and protected by law.

A legal right entails either a positive or negative duty on another. It entails a positive duty when the claim is that the other must perform an act. It is negative when the other person is restrained from doing an act. In general, this leads to two groups of legal rights: *personal rights* and *real rights*. A *personal right* is directed at a particular individual to do or refrain from doing an act. For example, X may have a right to claim that Y deliver a bicycle to him/her or that Y shall not interfere with his/her contractual relations. A *real right* is not directed at any particular person but is binding on all persons, requiring them all to refrain from doing an act. It is called 'real' because it arises from a person's exclusive interest in or benefit from a thing. All other persons are bound to respect this interest in or benefit from the thing in question. A typical real right is ownership of property. The owner of a piece of property is entitled to prevent all other persons from interfering with his/her enjoyment of the privileges of ownership.

Legal personality

Legal rights are enjoyed only by legal 'persons'. A human being is a person at law (therefore, a legal person). However, a human being is not the only person recognized by law. The law endows other entities with the capacity to acquire rights and incur obligations. A legal person is also defined as 'somebody who, or *something which*, can have legal rights and can also be bound by legal rights, i.e., be subject to legal duties.'[16]

Other entities endowed with legal personality are generally referred to as 'juristic' or 'artificial persons'. A company is the most notable example of a juristic person; even non-lawyers know that a company is a separate legal person from its shareholders and officials. It is appropriate to close this section on legal personality by referring to two brief passages from two leading South African legal textbooks.

Hahlo and Kahn say:

> There are two classes of persons in law: (i) 'natural persons', i.e., individual human beings who in modern law enjoy legal personality as a matter of course, and (ii) 'juristic' or 'artificial' persons, i.e., associations and bodies other than individual human beings upon which the law has seen fit to bestow the capacity for rights and duties.[17]

Wille's Principles of South African Law closed the issue of legal personality as follows:

> It must be emphasized that only persons have rights, and that things cannot have rights. There are rights of persons, and rights *over* things and *against* persons, but not rights *of* things. It follows that things have neither rights nor duties.

Notes

1. Phil Harris (2002) *An Introduction to Law*. Fifth edition. London: Butterworths, p. 3.
2. H.R. Hahlo and E. Kahn (1968) *The South African Legal System and its Background*. Cape Town: Juta and Co., pp. 3-4.
3. [1971], p. 83.
4. Per Ormerod J, p. 106.
5. 115 NY 506, 22 NE 188 (1889).
6. Voet, *Commentarius* 1.3.5.
7. See James Penner (1999) *McCoubrey and White's Textbook on Jurisprudence*. Third edition. Oxford: Blackstone Press Limited, p. 297.
8. See J.W. Harris (1997) *Legal Philosophies*. Second edition. London: Butterworths, p. 277.
9. 2001 (2) ZLR 457 (S), 490F-491B.
10. See Penner (1999), p. 299.
11. Hahlo and Kahn (1968), p. 26.
12. H. Hart (1992) *The Concept of Law*. Revised edition. Oxford: Oxford University Press, pp. 167-8.
13. See Lon L. Fuller (1969) *The Morality of Law*. Revised edition. New Haven and London: Yale University Press, pp. 3-4.
14. J.S. Mill (1993) *Utilitarianism, Liberty and Representative Government*. London: Everyman Paperbacks. pp. 72-3.
15. Dale Hutchison (ed.) (1991) *Wille's Principles of South African Law*. Eighth edition. Cape Town: Juta and Co., p. 38.
16. Ibid., p. 43. My italics.
17. Hahlo and Kahn (1968), p. 104.

2

Sources of Law

Legislation

Legislation is also referred to as statutory law and covers those rules of law made directly by the legislature. Each state has an organ responsible for law-making, and this is what is referred to as the legislature. The legislative authorities of the state promulgate law in various statutory forms such as Acts of Parliament, presidential decrees and ministerial regulations. One must be able to identify who the legislative authorities are. In Zimbabwe, the legislative authority is defined in Section 32 (1) of the Constitution as:

> The legislative authority of Zimbabwe shall vest in the legislature which shall consist of the President and Parliament.

Legislation by Parliament is embodied in a specialized legal document called an Act of Parliament.

It is only through these Acts that Parliament can make law. Parliament is entitled to delegate its law-making powers to the president, his/her ministers, local authorities and other state institutions.[1] When these authorities exercise this delegated power, they create what is called 'delegated legislation' (subsidiary legislation) that is embodied in specialized legal documents called 'statutory instruments'. Accordingly, there are two recognized forms of legislation in Zimbabwe: Acts of Parliament and statutory instruments.

A statutory instrument has the same legal status as an Act of Parliament, except that it must be consistent with the relevant Act of Parliament delegating the authority to make that statutory instrument. When it is consistent with the relevant Act, it is said to be *intra vires*. The relevant Act is called the 'parent Act' or the 'enabling Act'. A statutory instrument that is inconsistent with the enabling Act is said to be *ultra vires* and, for that reason, is void. For a statutory instrument to be *intra vires*, it must meet two requirements. First, it must be within the powers of the delegated authority. Second, it must not be grossly unreasonable.[2]

Under Zimbabwean law, there is one piece of legislation that is supreme and overrides all other laws to the contrary. This is the Constitution of Zimbabwe. The Constitution is itself an Act of Parliament but it is superior to all other Acts of Parliament. Section 3 of the Constitution says that '[t]his Constitution shall be the supreme law of Zimbabwe and any law which is inconsistent with it shall be void to the extent of the inconsistency'. Accordingly, even an Act of Parliament that has been duly passed and signed into law by the president is void if it is contrary to the Constitution.

The reason why any Constitution is given this special place in the hierarchy of laws is that, in principle, it is considered to be the word of the people themselves. In other words, it is legislated by the people. In many democratic systems of government, constitution-making involves the direct participation of the people through a referendum, thus reducing the role of the legislature to the mere formality of 'enacting the Constitution as approved by the people'. In countries where a referendum is not provided for, it is common for the enactment of a Constitution, or amendments to it, to require a special procedure such as approval by a two-thirds majority of the total membership of Parliament. The latter is the position in Zimbabwe, where the enactment of ordinary legislation merely requires approval by a majority of those 'present and voting'.

There is a hierarchy within the legislative source of law: the Constitution is supreme and is followed by ordinary Acts of Parliament and then by statutory instruments. If an Act of Parliament passes the constitutionality test, it is law for all purposes and cannot be nullified on any other grounds. A statutory instrument should pass both the *ultra vires* test and the constitutionality test.

Legislation may be cited in a variety of ways. Three main ways are:

1. By reference to the chapter, i.e., Labour Act (Chapter 28:01).
2. By reference to the short title and the calendar year in which it was enacted, for example, Labour Act, 1985.

3. By reference to the short title, the calendar year and its number in the calendar year in which it was enacted, for example, Labour Act, 1985 (Act No. 16 of 1985).

Zimbabwe adopts numbers one and three, with number three used only where there is no chapter allocation.

Statutory instruments are cited in only one way – they have no chapter number and reference is made to the title, the calendar year and its number in the year in which it was gazetted. This number refers to the order of gazetting, for example, Presidential Powers (Temporary Measures)(Labour Relations) Regulations, 1998 (SI 368A of 1998).[3]

Different countries have different modes of citation for statutes. For example, under the English system, no comma should be inserted between the word 'Act' and the calendar year, i.e., 'Insolvency Act 1986' and not 'Insolvency Act, 1986'.

An Act of Parliament does not fall into disuse. It comes to an end when it is repealed. This position is enshrined in the Constitution.

Apart from being repealed, there are two other ways in which an Act of Parliament may come to an end. The first is where it is found to be void for being inconsistent with the Constitution. The second is through the effluxion of time in situations where an Act is meant to be of limited duration. For example, a statute may provide that it shall remain in force until a given date.

There are conventions for the ways in which the contents of statutes are described. Key ones are shown in Table 1 overleaf.[4]

Common law

The term 'common law' has been used in three different senses, namely:

1. The law applicable to all people of a given society regardless of race, tribe and sex.

2. As part of a classification of legal systems which have the influence of the English common law as distinct from those which have been termed civil law systems with a Roman law basis.

3. As that portion of the law which is not derived from legislation and emanates from a collection of principles made by judges in the course of resolving issues brought before the courts.[5]

The third sense is the most appropriate starting point to an understanding of the 'common law' as a source of law. It is important to distinguish

SOURCES OF LAW

Instrument	First division	Second division	Third division	Fourth division
Act	Section 1	sub-Section (1)	paragraph (a)	sub-paragraph (i)
Bill	Clause 1	sub-Section 1	paragraph (a)	sub-paragraph (i)
Schedule to an Act	Paragraph 1	sub-paragraph 1	sub-paragraph (a)	
Statutory instruments (in general)	Section 1	sub-Section 1	paragraph (a)	
Statutory instruments (Rules, e.g., Rules of Court)	Rule 1	sub-rule 1	paragraph (a)	
Convention/Treaty	Article 1	paragraph 1		

Table 1: Key conventions for describing the contents of statutes

between English law and Zimbabwean and South African law in this regard. Under English law, the 'common law' is accurately described by the third sense above. Under Zimbabwean and South African law, the common law is made up of two components of non-statutory law, namely, (i) a collection of rules and principles made by judges in previous cases, and (ii) rules and principles contained in that portion of the body of law called 'Roman Dutch law' that is not reflected in any previous court decision. This understanding of the term 'common law' under our law will be clear following an explanation of the nature of Roman Dutch law.

Under English law, it is accurate to refer to the common law as 'judge-made law'. Under Zimbabwean law, only a portion of the common law is necessarily judge-made. Another expression commonly encountered in this context is 'judicial precedent'. This expression is synonymous with judge-made law, except that it may be used where the expression 'judge-made law' would not apply. This one respect is in the area of statutory interpretation. When a court ascribes a meaning to a given provision of an enactment, that meaning may bind future courts. This situation is covered by the expression 'judicial precedent' but it cannot be described as 'judge-made law'.

Although the expressions 'judge-made law' and 'judicial precedent' are synonymous (except for the one instance referred to above), in English law the common law is almost exclusively based on judicial precedent.

Historically, judges in England decided the first law cases by applying general principles of justice, common sense and morality. Gradually, they began to follow their previous decisions under the doctrine of *stare decisis* (to stand by the decision). Over time, the body of law founded on previous decisions became sufficiently broad in its scope to justify the rule that all rulings had to be based on previous decisions. This body of law is what is called the 'common law' in the English legal system. In an exceptional case, there may be no relevant previous case. In such a case, a court cannot say: 'There is no law in point and therefore the dispute cannot be resolved'. Rather, it must establish the common law by applying what may be termed fundamental principles of justice and fairness.

In countries that were colonized, including those in Africa, the colonial power imposed a Western legal system. As a rule, the imposed legal system required the colony to adopt some specified foreign laws as at the time of the imposition. The 'common law' of a colony was therefore made up of two components: (i) the principles of law contained in the foreign law as at the time of imposition, and (ii) law derived from judicial precedent developed after the date of imposition. This was and is the situation in Zimbabwe. Section 89 of the Constitution of Zimbabwe states:

> Subject to the provisions of any law for the time being in force in Zimbabwe relating to the application of African customary law, the law to be administered by the Supreme Court, the High Court and by any courts in Zimbabwe subordinate to the High Court shall be the law in force in the Colony of the Cape of Good Hope on 10th June, 1891, as modified by subsequent legislation having in Zimbabwe the force of law.

A brief history of Roman Dutch law

The law applying at the Cape of Good Hope on 10 June 1891 was largely based on Roman Dutch law. Roman Dutch law is a fusion of Roman law and medieval Dutch law. This fusion occurred in Holland (now part of the Netherlands) over a considerable period of time and was completed by the end of the sixteenth century. The term 'Roman Dutch law' (Roomsch–Hollandsch Recht) appears to have been coined by a seventeenth-century Dutch jurist, Simon Van Leeuwen, who used it as the title of his main book, *Roomsch Hollandsch Recht*, which was published in 1664. Holland, whose inhabitants were mainly tribes of Germanic origin, was conquered and occupied by the Romans under the Emperor, Julius Caesar. Although this foreign occupation lasted for approximately five hundred years, the people living in Holland were allowed to follow their own customs and way of life, except in situations that the Romans regarded as either criminal or unacceptable. However, it was inevitable that the culture and laws of the Romans would come to exert a great deal of influence upon them. Hahlo and Kahn describe this situation as follows:

> In conformity with their usual practice in dealing with conquered territories, the Romans did not attempt to force Roman law and institutions on their new subjects. Five hundred years of Roman rule could not, however, fail to leave their impression on laws of the Germanic tribes. The superstructure of government and administration was Roman. Roman garrison towns were founded and large Roman country estates established. Roman civil servants, officers and businessmen constituted the ruling class. As labour tenants on Roman estates, as domestic servants in Roman households, as soldiers in the Roman army and clerks in Roman business firms the members of the 'subject' races picked up the ideas of their masters and took them back to their tribes. The history of the late Roman Empire was characterized by the Romanisation of the provinces and by the barbarisation of Rome.[6]

Thus, the first reception of Roman laws in Holland took place through the process, described in the above passage, of gradual infiltration. With the collapse of Roman rule in AD 476 the reception of Roman law took a new form which involved resorting to Roman law in situations where customary law failed to provide an answer. Bit by bit, the local customary law was reconstructed in the light of Roman law. However, the pace was very slow and the results were not substantial until the fourteenth and fifteenth centuries. *Wille's Principles of South African Law* completes the story as follows:

> In the fourteenth and fifteenth centuries the material prosperity of Holland advanced considerably, owing largely to commercial and social intercourse with other European countries, and as a consequence more fully developed laws were required to meet the new conditions. It was about this time that Roman law began to influence the local law ... [in] the Netherlands, when it was becoming clear that the local Dutch laws were not sufficiently developed to suit the conditions of the country, the more detailed principles of the Roman law were turned to and applied by the rulers, by the courts and by the people. At first as patterns of wisdom and equity, and in the course of time through custom as laws, the greater portion of the Roman law was adopted, and it is generally accepted that by the end of the sixteenth century this process was complete.[7]

It was easy to access Roman law because it had been compiled into one encyclopaedic collection called *Corpus Juris Civilis* in AD 533 by Emperor Justinian. Roman Dutch law is a product of this fusion of Dutch customs and Roman law. By the end of the sixteenth century, it was this special brand of law that was the law of Holland. In 1652, Jan van Riebeeck and his group of Dutch settlers took charge of the Cape of Good Hope. They brought with them, and introduced, the law as it applied at that time in Holland, which was Roman Dutch law, and all legislation in force at the time. Roman Dutch law was contained in judicial decisions and published treatises on law written by Dutch jurists. From 1652 onwards, and indeed up to this day, the nucleus of the law of Zimbabwe and South Africa, as well as that of Botswana, Lesotho, Namibia and Swaziland, has remained Roman Dutch.

The law introduced at the Cape in 1652 underwent some significant changes after 1795. In that year, the British took over the Cape from the Dutch. They did not replace Roman Dutch law, but English law began to influence some legal aspects.

By 10 June 1891, the law applicable at the Cape was Roman Dutch law with substantial English law graftings. This is why Section 89 of the Constitution of Zimbabwe refers to 'the law in force in the colony of the Cape of Good Hope' and not 'the Roman Dutch law in force'. Nevertheless, it is accurate to say that the basis of our common law is Roman Dutch law as long as it is borne in mind that some considerable aspects of our common law are derived from English law.

There are two main sources of Roman Dutch law: judicial decisions and the writings of the old Dutch jurists (so-called legal treatises). If we were to place ourselves at the Cape of Good Hope on 10 June 1891, we would find the common law applicable from (i) judicial decisions up to that date and (ii) the writings of the old Dutch jurists. It is this body of law we are required to apply by Section 89 of the Constitution. That body of law is binding on the courts as part of our common law.

Ever since 10 June 1891 there have been countless judicial decisions explaining our common law. These and the pre-10 June 1891 judicial decisions, together with the writings of the old Dutch jurists, constitute the common law of Zimbabwe. In ascertaining the common law, one has to look for relevant *judicial* decisions. If there are none, one must turn to the treatises of the old Dutch jurists. Of these men, there are several who set out the principles of Roman Dutch law. The most important are (i) Hugo Grotius (Hugo de Groot) (1583–1645), who wrote *Inleiding*; (ii) Johannes Voet (1647–1713), who wrote *Commentarius ad Pandectas* (1698); (iii) Simon van Leeuwen (1625–1682), who wrote *Censura Forensis* (1662) and *Het Roomsch Hollandsch Reich* (1664); (iv) Dionysius Godefried van der Keessel (1738–1816), who wrote *Theses Selectae*; and (v) Johannes van der Linden (1756–1835), who wrote the *Practical Handbook* (1806).

Where there is a difference of opinion among the various jurists, Roman law becomes relevant. Although Roman law is not a source of our common law, as it is different to Roman Dutch law, where there is a difference of opinion, the opinion supported by Roman law is preferred. If neither is supported by Roman law, or where the Roman law is itself not clear, the opinion to be preferred is that which is backed by more practical convenience.

The insertion of the date 10 June 1891 in Section 89 of the Constitution of Zimbabwe is intended to ensure that the courts of law are bound by any rules and principles of law which were adopted at the Cape of Good Hope at that time, regardless of whether they were pure Roman Dutch law or English law, or even whether they are now considered 'wrong'. The issue in each case is what law was applicable as at that date.

Unfortunately, our courts do not seem alive to this logical approach. Thus, in *Book v Davidson*, the Zimbabwean Supreme Court suddenly abandoned English law on the onus of proof in restraint of trade cases in favour of South African law without ascertaining 'the law in force in the colony of the Cape of Good Hope on 10 June 1891'.[8] The law on the issues in question was English. Dumbutshena CJ said:

> Mr Robinson contended that it was not wise to abandon English law which has been consistently followed by the courts in this country as the law applicable in Zimbabwe in cases involving contracts in restraint of trade. Should this court decide that the correct approach is the one urged upon us by Mr Robinson, the fact that the South African Appellate Division had decided otherwise on the question of onus will not matter because the decisions of the Appellate Division are not binding on this court. This court cannot, however, lightly ignore the decision in *Magna Alloys and Research v Ellis* because Zimbabwe is a Roman Dutch law country. Decisions of a court in another Roman Dutch law jurisdiction have, in related cases, very persuasive authority. It is therefore the duty of the court to weigh on the scales of justice, the approaches of English law and Roman Dutch law.[9]

This last sentence, where it is said to be the duty of the court 'to weigh on the scales of justice the approaches of English law and Roman Dutch law' has no legal foundation whatsoever. Further, these words are difficult to reconcile with the earlier statement that a Zimbabwean court 'cannot lightly ignore' South African decisions 'because Zimbabwe is a Roman Dutch common law country'. The proper approach should have been for the court to ascertain the law applicable on 10 June 1891, which, while largely Roman Dutch, may have been adopted from English law. With this approach, there is no scope 'to weigh on the scales of justice, English law and Roman Dutch law'.

Given that the common law develops through previous judicial decisions, some critical points need to be made about this process. It is not everything in a previous case that is binding on a future court. For a proposition to be binding, it must meet the following requirements:

- It should be a proposition of law and not a proposition of fact.
- The proposition must be part of the *ratio decidendi* (reason for the decision). The *ratio decidendi* is the principle of law upon which the decision is based. However, in a judgment, it is common for a judge to make statements of law in passing which do not form part of the reason for the decision. A statement of such a nature is called *obiter dictum*

[plural form being *obiter dicta*]. The distinction between the *ratio decidendi* and *obiter dictum* is central to the operation of the common law. If the other requirements are satisfied, it is only the *ratio decidendi* that is binding on a future court, while an *obiter dictum* has no binding status but only what may be termed 'persuasive value'.

- There must be no material differences between the previous case and the case in question. Where there is a material difference between the two cases, the previous case is 'distinguished' and the precedent made not binding. Whether or not a difference is 'material' depends upon the circumstances of each situation and no test can be formulated.

Smith and Bailey on the Modern English Legal System says the following about 'distinguishing':

> A precedent, whether persuasive or binding, need not be applied or followed if it can be distinguished, i.e., there is a material distinction between the facts of the precedent case and the case in question. What counts as a material distinction is obviously crucial. The judge in the later case is expected to explain why the distinction is such as to justify the application of a different rule. If the distinction is spurious, the judge may be criticized or reversed or, if the case distinguished is generally regarded as a bad precedent, applauded for his or her boldness. There is no test or set of tests for whether a distinction is legally relevant, it all depends upon the circumstances of the case.[10]

- It should be binding on the court deciding the case in question. There is a hierarchy of courts. A court is only bound by a precedent if the precedent emanates from a court which, in terms of hierarchy, is of a higher level. There are, however, some exceptions even to this statement. The Supreme Court of Zimbabwe is the highest court of the land. Its precedents bind all the lower courts. The High Court binds all the lower courts to the extent that its precedent is not inconsistent with any precedent of the Supreme Court. The High Court itself is not bound by its previous decisions, but is bound by decisions of the Supreme Court. The Supreme Court is not bound by its previous decisions, although it generally follows them.

This position is aptly captured by the Practice Directive issued by the Supreme Court in 1981. It reads as follows:

> This court considers it of importance that there be a degree of certainty upon which people can rely in the conduct of their affairs. Precedent is an important factor upon which to decide both what the law is and how it is to apply in particular cases. It also serves as a proper starting point for any development of the law. Nevertheless, particularly in a changing society, it is essential for the courts to have some flexibility so as not to restrict unduly its power to develop

the law in proper cases to meet changing conditions and injustice in particular cases. For the future, this court while treating its past decisions and those of its predecessors as normally binding, will depart from a previous decision when it appears right to do so, applying the principles generally acceptable under the law.[11]

This statement followed, almost verbatim, that issued by the House of Lords in England in 1966, thus reflecting what appears to be the practice of almost all the highest courts of legal systems of the world. The 1966 statement from the House of Lords reads as follows:

> Their Lordships regard the use of precedent as an indispensable foundation upon which to decide what is the law and its application to individual cases. It provides at least some degree of certainty upon which individuals can rely in the conduct of their affairs, as well as a basis for orderly development of legal rules.
>
> Their Lordships nevertheless recognize that too rigid adherence to precedent may lead to injustice in a particular case and also unduly restrict the proper development of the law. They propose, therefore, to modify their present practice and, while treating former decisions of this House as normally binding, to depart from a previous decision when it appears right to do so.
>
> In this connection they will bear in mind the danger of disturbing retrospectively the basis on which contracts, settlements of property and fiscal arrangements have been entered into and also the special need for certainty as to the criminal law.[12]

It is only the superior courts that can create precedent in the sense in which it is referred to here. A Magistrates Court does not create binding precedent and is itself not bound by any of its previous decisions. It is, however, expected to be consistent in its decision-making. A decision of a Magistrates Court is not precedent for lower courts such as Small-Claims Courts and local courts on customary law. Regarding tribunals created by statute, the general rule is that they do not create precedent binding on themselves except in one situation. This situation is where there is a hierarchy of tribunals, in which case an appellate tribunal creates binding precedent for a lower tribunal. A good example is the Labour Court established in terms of the Labour Act (Chapter 28:01). Its decisions create binding precedent for labour officers and arbitrators deciding labour matters at a lower level.

Our courts are not bound by any decisions of foreign courts. However, because of the nature of our common law, decisions of the highest courts in South Africa and England are very persuasive authority.

The Zimbabwe Supreme Court has had occasion to depart from its previous decisions. Two examples will suffice. In *United Bottlers (Pvt.) Ltd v Murwisi*, the Supreme Court held that Section 3 of SI371/85 (Termination of Employment Regulations) gave a labour relations officer only two choices: either to authorize the dismissal of an employee or to order his/her reinstatement.[13] It emphasized that under that Section, the option to order the payment of damages in lieu of reinstatement did not exist. A year later, in *Hama v National Railways of Zimbabwe*, it departed from this decision.[14] It held that the position in *United Bottlers (Pvt.) Ltd v Murwisi* where a labour relations officer had only these two choices was incorrect. There was an additional option for a labour relations officer to order the payment of damages as an alternative to reinstatement.

In *Katekwe v Muchabaiwa*, the Supreme Court held that the effect of Legal Age of Majority Act was that the father of an African woman who had attained the age of majority (18 years) no longer had the right to sue for seduction damages in respect of his daughter.[15] The basis of this decision was that under customary law, a woman was a perpetual minor and so could not sue on her own for seduction damages. By conferring majority status on a woman, the Legal Age of Majority Act gave the woman in question the right to sue on her own for seduction damages. However, in *Magaya v Magaya*, it held that *Katekwe v Muchabaiwa* had been wrongly decided.[16] Its new position was that the reason why a woman could not sue for seduction damages was not because of her 'minority' status but because of the very nature of African society. Accordingly, the conferring of majority status by the Legal Age of Majority Act did not entitle a woman to exercise rights not accorded to her by customary law. For instance, she could not sue for seduction damages despite the enactment of the Legal Age of Majority Act.

Advantages of precedent

The doctrine of precedent has several advantages. They are summarized as follows:

> The advantages of a principle of *stare decisis* are many. It enables the citizen, if necessary with the aid of practicing lawyers, to plan his private and professional activities with some degree of assurance as to their legal effects; it prevents the dislocation of rights, particularly contractual and proprietary ones, created in the belief of an existing rule of law; it cuts down the prospect of litigation, it keeps the weaker judge along right and rational paths, drastically limiting the play allowed to partiality, caprice or prejudice, thereby not only securing justice in the instance but also retaining public confidence in the

judicial machine through like being dealt with alike, and it conserves the time of the courts and reduces the cost of law suits .... Certainty, predictability, reliability, equality, uniformity, convenience, these are the principal advantages to be gained by a legal system from the principle of *stare decisis*.[17]

Hosten added his own voice in these words:

The idea of precedent suggests the resolution of questions today in the same manner as they were decided yesterday either because it is convenient to do so or because it is intended to profit from the accumulated wisdom of the past, or because one can assure certainty or for honouring traditions. Adherence to precedents is characteristic of all developed systems.[18]

The obvious disadvantage of precedent is lack of adequate flexibility to change the law to meet changing times and situations.

Custom

Customs are rules that become binding in the course of time through observance by the community in question. They are not necessarily written down. In other words, the community becomes accustomed to regulating its relationship in a particular way, with many of its members regarding that particular way of doing things as legally binding.

There are two types of custom:

1. General custom, which applies in such fields of law as banking, commercial law, international trade law and so on.
2. African customary law, which regulates the life of indigenous Africans.

General custom

As regards general custom, a custom is legally binding if it satisfies four requirements:

1. It is reasonable.
2. It is long-binding, i.e., clearly established.
3. It is uniformly observed.
4. It is certain.

A good illustration of the use of custom as a source of law is the case of *Van Breda v Jacobs*.[19] In this case, the court upheld a custom in the fishing trade whereby persons involved in fishing could lay a claim to fish in the sea not yet captured by their nets as long as they were in the line of their nets.

The onus is on the person who relies on the existence of a custom to prove each of the four requirements specified above. Problems are likely to arise with some of the requirements. For example, given the varying conceptions of reasonableness, different courts may come to opposite conclusions about whether or not an alleged custom is reasonable. According to Voet, a custom is not reasonable if it is *contra bonos mores* (contrary to public morality).[20] Regarding the requirement that the custom be long-binding, in the sense of having been observed for a long time, there is no minimum period except to say that 'the custom must have existed for a sufficient length of time to have become generally known'.[21] One such example is the custom of bankers charging interest on overdrawn accounts, a custom that has been given the force of law.

African customary law

African customary law is a specialized form of law in Zimbabwe. Zimbabwe has what is termed a *dual legal system*, being comprised of general law (common law and statute) and African customary law. This means that in certain matters, there is a potential application of two different systems of law with different legal consequences.

A person may or may not be governed by African customary law. Thus, X may be governed by customary law and thereby subjected to the consequences of that law while Y may be governed by general law with different consequences. This is what a dual legal system entails. There are also matters over which some questions are governed by customary law and not general law.

Section 89 of the Constitution of Zimbabwe sanctions the existence of this dual legal system. Whether or not customary law applies in a particular case is governed by the provisions of the Customary Law and Local Courts Act (Chapter 7:05).

In terms of this Act, customary law applies under two circumstances, namely:

1. Where the provisions of a relevant statute say so.
2. In the absence of a relevant statute, by applying the 'choice of law formula' in Section 3 of the Act.

A statute may specifically provide that customary law shall apply in a given set of circumstances. The best example was the old Section 13 (now repealed) of the Customary Marriages Act (Chapter 5:07) that provided as follows:

Marriage between Africans in terms of the Marriage Act shall not affect the property of the spouses, which shall be held and shall devolve according to customary law.

There are very few statutes that impose the application of customary law, thus in the majority of cases reliance has to be placed on applying the provisions of Section 3. An analysis of these provisions yields several interesting features.

First, customary law applies in civil matters only. It does not apply in criminal cases. In *S v Matyenyika & Another*, the High Court dealt with a case involving the crime of incest (prohibited sexual intercourse between persons in certain defined relationships).[22] It set aside the conviction of the two cousins who, according to customary law, were prohibited from having sexual relations. There was no similar prohibition under the general law (common law). The Magistrates Court had convicted them on the basis of the prohibitions of customary law. In other words, it applied customary law to determine whether or not the crime of incest had been committed. The High Court set aside the conviction on the basis that customary law did not apply in criminal matters.

Malaba J (as he then was) said:

> Customary law is therefore not the appropriate test to apply in deciding whether the crime of incest has been committed or not .... Customary law should therefore not have influenced the prosecution in deciding whether to charge the accused with the crime of incest, nor should it have influenced the magistrates in deciding that the crime had been committed by the accused.[23]

Second, customary law applies where the plaintiff(s) and defendant(s) agree that it should. The only point to note here is that the agreement must be genuine. The agreement may be either express or implied, i.e., where, with regard to the nature of the case and the surrounding circumstances, it is reasonable to assume that the parties are in agreement.

Third, where there is no agreement (whether expressly or by implication), the courts may impose the application of customary law, but only on the basis that it 'is just and proper'. In deciding this, the Act requires the Court to consider the 'surrounding circumstances'. These are defined as including (i) the mode of life of the parties, (ii) the subject matter of the case, (iii) the parties' knowledge of customary law and/or general law, and (iv) the closeness of the case to general law or customary law. The court makes an overall judgment of whether or not it is 'just and proper' after weighing up these four aspects. In general, the decision is at the discretion of the trial court. An appeal court will not interfere with the decision, even where it might form a different opinion on the facts. It will only intervene and change the decision of the trial court if, having regard to the facts, the conclusion reached is one that no reasonable court should have come to.

A case that illustrates the application of customary law where there is no agreement between the parties and where the court imposes it on the basis that it is 'just and proper' is *Lopez v Nxumalo*.[24] Here, the appellant was a white Portuguese man and the respondent was a black Zimbabwean woman. The appellant had seduced the respondent's daughter and the respondent wished to sue him for seduction damages under customary law. The appellant contended that he knew no African custom and was not acquainted with African customary law. He thus sought to have the matter dealt with under general law and not customary law, arguing that the community court had no jurisdiction to hear the matter. The community court rejected his arguments and held that customary law applied and therefore that it had jurisdiction. The appellant then appealed to the Supreme Court but his appeal was thrown out. The Supreme Court noted that the fact that the appellant had no knowledge of African custom and customary law was merely one of the factors taken into account. That factor had been weighed against the fact that the respondent did not understand general law and that she and her daughter lived a life guided by customary law. It further noted that the community court had weighed up all these factors and come to the conclusion that it was just and proper for customary law to apply. Consequently, it found no basis for interfering with that conclusion.

Fourth, the choice of law formula in Section 3 applies 'unless the justice of the case otherwise requires'. The expression 'unless the justice of the case otherwise requires' has significance. It means that where the choice of law process yields the application of customary law, but it has been established that the content of customary law would attain an unjust resolution of the matter, general law, not customary law, must be applied, even where the parties have agreed that customary law should apply. This position was clearly articulated by Chatikobo J in *Matibiri v Kumire*:

> In my view, the only logical construction to place on the phrase 'unless the justice of the case otherwise requires' is that if the application of customary law does not conduce to the attainment of justice then common law should apply .... The phrase, 'unless the justice of the case otherwise requires', has remained in all Acts passed by Parliament, including the current one .... What emerges is that for the one hundred years during which customary law has co-existed

with Roman Dutch law, it has always been provided through legislation that where the customary choice of law rules were found to be inapplicable to the just decision of any matter in controversy, then in that event, resort should be had to common law principles.[25]

This approach was endorsed by the Supreme Court in *Chapeyama v Matende & Another*.[26] In this case, the appellant and respondent were married under customary law. The marriage was not registered under the Customary Marriages Act (Chapter 5:07) and was therefore what is termed an 'unregistered customary law union'. They lived together for seven years, having fallen in love when they were in Grade Seven. They had two children and had acquired considerable property through their joint efforts. The property included a house in Harare that was registered in both their names. The husband terminated the marriage relationship and sought an order from the courts to have the respondent's name deleted from the registration certificate pertaining to the house. The respondent opposed the order and counter-claimed for a fair distribution of the matrimonial assets, including the house. The court was of the view that, in general, where parties are married according to customary law, their rights and duties are governed by customary law. According to customary law, the respondent, notwithstanding having contributed substantially to the matrimonial assets, was only entitled to the *amai* and *maoko* property and not to a general distribution of matrimonial property.[27] On the face of it, customary law yielded clear injustice. The court held that this was a proper case to resort to the 'justice of the case' and refused to apply customary law.

The facts of *Matibiri v Kumire* were that the parties were married in terms of customary law and the marriage had not been solemnized. The marriage was subsequently dissolved in accordance with customary law. Although the wife had contributed to the matrimonial property, which included a house, she was left with goods of very little value. She brought an application seeking fair distribution of matrimonial assets. The court applied the choice of law rules. It established that there was no express agreement between the parties that customary law should apply. It also concluded that there was no basis to draw the inference from the nature of the case and the surrounding circumstances that the parties had agreed that customary law should apply. On the assumption that the facts pointed to the application of customary law, mainly because the parties were married under customary law, the court considered the remedies under that law. It noted that 'upon dissolution of an unregistered customary union, the property acquired by the parties during the union becomes the property of the husband unless it can be clarified as *amai* or *maoko* property'. It considered this to be an unjust result as it left the wife without a remedy. On the basis of the expression 'unless the justice of the case otherwise requires', it refused to apply customary law and resorted to general law.

In *Mtuda v Ndudzo* the parties were also married in terms of customary law but their union was unregistered. On dissolution of the marriage, the wife sought a fair distribution of the matrimonial property. Garwe J appears to have applied the 'just and proper' basis to reach the conclusion that, in general, the law to apply in the distribution of property in an unregistered customary union is customary law.[28] However, on the basis of the justice of the particular case, he refused to apply customary law as that would have entitled the wife only to the *maoko* property. He applied general law and found a basis for the wife's claims under the principles of unjust enrichment.

The interplay between customary law and general law in Zimbabwe has been problematic. This is best illustrated by cases involving the rights of women under customary law. In *Katekwe v Muchabaiwa*, the Supreme Court held that the father of an African female who had reached the age of 18 no longer had a right to sue for seduction damages under customary law in respect of his daughter.[29] On the basis that the Legal Age of Majority Act had changed the status of women even under customary law, it was argued before, and accepted by, the Supreme Court that the reason why women could not sue on their own under customary law was because they were regarded as perpetual minors. The Legal Age of Majority Act gave them majority status on reaching 18 and therefore bestowed on them rights they could not enjoy under customary law.

This reasoning was followed in *Chihowa v Mangwende*, where it was held that one of the consequences of the Legal Age of Majority Act was that a woman who had attained the age of 18 could be validly appointed as the heiress of her father's estate under customary law, and with the same rights and duties as those which devolve upon a male heir.[30] The position was changed in *Vareta v Vareta*.[31] In this case, it was held that the eldest son was the natural heir of the father's estate even if there was an older female sibling and that the situation had not been affected by the Legal Age of Majority Act. *Chihowa v Mangwende* was then restricted to cases where there was no male heir. In *Murisa v Murisa* the Supreme

Court confirmed the customary law rule that a wife cannot inherit from her husband's estate.[32]

In *Magaya v Magaya* the Supreme Court delivered a bombshell.[33] It held that *Katekwe v Muchabaiwa* had been wrongly decided. The Legal Age of Majority Act did not affect rights and duties under customary law. According to *Magaya v Magaya*, women have no rights of inheritance under customary law, not because they are minors but because they are women in an African society.

In *Jena v Nyemba*, the Supreme Court set out the proprietary consequences of a marriage under customary law in the following terms:

> In African law and custom, property acquired during a marriage becomes the husband's property whether acquired by him or his wife. To this rule, there are a few exceptions.[34]

The main exception is that the wife is entitled to her *amai* and *maoko* property. *Amai* property is 'that category of property [which] comprises the livestock and its increase which accrues to a woman as a result of her daughter's marriage and pregnancy'. *Maoko* property covers all property acquired by the woman through her personal labours.[35]

A different type of issue where customary law is still relevant is the succession to chieftaincy. This is governed exclusively by customary law, which is recognized by the Constitution of Zimbabwe. Section 111 (2) requires the president, when appointing a chief, to 'give due consideration to the customary principles of succession of the tribes people over which the chief will preside'. This notwithstanding, several disputes over customary law rules of succession have been heard in the courts.[36]

Is customary law a bag of rules discovered as a matter of fact or is it a living body of rules that can be developed by the courts? The courts seem to have taken the view that customary law is a matter of fact.[37] In *Jengwa v Jengwa*, Gillespie J had this observation to make:

> A judicial finding that customary law has changed to permit an equitable division of marital property may be unattainable, depending on the judicial status of customary law. If its exigencies are regarded as a question of fact, being immutable mores discovered by expert evidence, then a court cannot purport to develop customary law. If it be regarded as a living system of law, changing with the changing times, then judicial development of its principles may be appropriate. That, however, is beyond the scope of this judgment.[38]

In *Mutaisi v Muzondo*, the High Court accepted the concept of customary law as being a matter of fact and adopted the following passage from Hamnett:

> Customary law emerges from what people do or more accurately – from what people believe they ought to do, rather than from what a class of legal specialists consider they should do or believe .... The ultimate test is not 'what does this judge say?' but rather 'what do the participants in the law regard as the rights and duties that apply to them? The real task of the customary jurist is to answer this last question, not to apply deductive or analytical reasoning to a set of professionally formulated legal concepts .... Customary law can be regarded as a set of norms which the actors in a social situation abstract from practice and which they invest with binding authority'.[39]

As the above examples show, the application of customary law depends on determining what it is that the community in question treats as binding customs. In this respect, the main method of ascertaining it is through expert witnesses on African customary law.[40] These witnesses may be either academics or elders in the community in question who have knowledge of the customary practices.[41] The court may also rely on textbooks on customary law written by persons of established repute who have vast knowledge on the subject, and without putting the contents of such books to an expert witness for confirmation.[42] Where reliance is placed on a textbook that does not meet this description, the contents thereof must be confirmed by an expert witness.[43]

Authoritative texts

Authoritative texts refer to writings by leading authorities in the field of law. As already noted, treatises written by Roman Dutch jurists are authoritative sources of Roman Dutch law and are treated as such in the courts. They are regarded as sources under the heading of common law because of their special nature.

Reference must also be made to modern textbooks and scholarly articles or publications. Though these have no inherent authority of their own, they may be regarded as very persuasive sources of law where neither legislation nor case law is in point, or where they are explaining a legal point which is not clearly covered in legislation or case law.

The persuasive nature of an opinion of an author depends, *inter alia*, on the standing of the author in the field of law in question, the reputation of the author among judges, the scholarly level of the piece of work involved and the degree to which the nature of the presentation is convincing.

Law reports

An essential component of a system based on precedent is one where these precedents are reported. Judgments from the superior courts (the High Court and the Supreme Court) are required by law to be in writing. This also applies to courts lower than the superior courts. Once a superior court has delivered a judgment, it is made available to the public.

Most countries, Zimbabwe included, have a system in which all judgments delivered by the superior courts are scrutinized by legal experts with a view to selecting *some* of them for publication in official law reports.

A judgment that is not selected for publication is described as 'unreported' and that which is published is described as 'reported'. However, an unreported judgment has the same precedent value as a reported judgment. In Zimbabwe, the official series of reported judgments is called the *Zimbabwe Law Reports*. The decision as to which judgments are reported in the *Zimbabwe Law Reports* is made by a group of self-appointed editors.

A full law report usually includes the following details: names of the parties, the court in which the case was decided, name(s) of the judge(s), date or dates of hearing, list of cases discussed or cited, names of the lawyers, an indication of whether the judgment was reserved by the inclusion of the expression *'curia advisari vult'* (the court wishes to consider the matter) and a headnote (a summary of the decision which is prepared by the reporter). Zimbabwe has only one set of official law reports, but other countries have several sets.

A passage from Michael Zander's *The Law-Making Process* sums up the issue of the law reports in the following terms:

> One of the essential elements in a system based on precedent is some tolerably efficient method for making the precedents available to those wishing to discover the law. An unreported decision is technically of precisely the same authority as one that is reported, but decisions that are unreported have at least until very recently been more or less inaccessible to all but scholars. It is through law reporting that the common law is available to the profession and anyone else wishing to know the law.[44]

Notes

1. See Section 32 (2) of the Constitution of Zimbabwe.
2. These two aspects are discussed later in Chapter 5.

3. SI 368A/98.
4. Adapted from Hahlo and Kahn (1968), pp. 175-6.
5. See Glanville Williams (1982) Learning the Law. London: Sweet and Maxwell, p. 24.
6. Ibid., pp. 485-6.
7. *Wille's Principles of South African Law* (1991), pp. 20-1.
8. 1988 (1) *ZLR* 365 (S).
9. 1984 (4) SA 874 (A), p. 375.
10. See S.H. Bailey and M.J. Gunn (1996) *Smith and Bailey on the Modern English Legal System*. Third edition. Andover: Sweet and Maxwell, p. 448.
11. 1981 ZLR 417.
12. 1966 (1) *WLR* 1234.
13. 1995 (1) *ZLR* 246 (S).
14. 1996 (1) *ZLR* 664 (S).
15. 1984 (2) *ZLR* 112 (S).
16. 1999 (1) *ZLR* 100 (S).
17. Hahlo and Kahn (1968), pp. 214-15.
18. W.J. Hosten et al. (1995) *Introduction to South African Law and Legal Theory*. Second edition. London: Butterworths, p. 386.
19. 1921 AD 330.
20. See Voet, 1.3.28.
21. See *Wille's Principles of South African Law* (1991), p. 9.
22. 1996 (2) *ZLR* 536 (H).
23. See 540B-F.
24. SC-115-85.
25. 2000 (1) *ZLR* 492 (N), 497E-498B.
26. 2000 (2) *ZLR* 356 (5).
27. *Amai* property is that which a woman derives from the marriage of her daugter, such as the cow that is given to the mother of the bride as part of *roora/lobola*. *Maoko* property is that which comes out of the woman's own technical work, such as the proceeds from selling handcrafts she has made.
28. 2000 (1) *ZLR* 710 (H), p. 713F.
29. 1984 (1) *ZLR* 112.
30. 1987 (1) *ZLR* 290.
31. SC 126 1990.
32. 1992 (1) *ZLR* 167.
33. 1999 (1) *ZLR* 100.
34. 1986 (1) *ZLR* 138 (S), p. 142.
35. Ibid., p. 142.
36. See, for example, *Ruzane v Paradzai and Anor*, 1991 (1) ZLR 273 (SC); *Chipfuyamiti v Nyajina and Anor*, 1992 (2) ZLR 148 (H); *Rushwaya v Minister of Local Government and Anor*, 1987 (1) ZLR 15 (S).
37. See *Magaya v Magaya*; *Vareta v Vareta*; and *Chapeyema v Matende*.

38. 1999 (2) *ZLR* 121 (H), 128E.
39. 1999 (2) *ZLR* 435 (H), p. 437.
40. See *Madondo v Mkushi* 1985 (2) *ZLR* 198 (SC), 203A.
41. Ibid.
42. See *Ruzana v Paradzai and Anor* 1991 (1) *ZLR* 273 (SC), 278G.
43. Ibid.
44. Michael Zander (1994) *The Law-Making Process*. Fourth edition. London: Butterworths, p. 239.

3

Divisions of the Law

Criminal law versus civil law

A crime is a wrong punishable by the state, and the main object of criminal law is punishment of the offender(s). A civil wrong is a wrong against another person, and the main object of civil law is to compensate the victim for the harm suffered. Although a crime is a wrong against an individual, it is considered a wrong against the state and it is the latter which has the prerogative of prosecuting. In exceptional cases, a private prosecution is permitted.

Every legal system decides which wrongs against individuals are to be regarded as wrongs against the state and therefore punishable by the state. It is clear that a wrong becomes a crime solely because of the decision by the legal system that it be regarded as such. This is why a crime in one society may not be a crime in another. For example, while homosexual practices are regarded as criminal in Zimbabwe, they are not in South Africa.

A wrong may be both a crime and a civil wrong. Whereas virtually all crimes are civil wrongs, the reverse is not the case. Most civil wrongs are not crimes. Examples of civil wrongs include breach of contract, delicts (defamation, assaults) and trespass.

The prerogative of the state to pursue a criminal prosecution does not affect the civil remedies available to a person who has been wronged. Where the wrong is both a crime and a civil wrong, it is permissible to institute both proceedings at the same time or one after the other. The result in one case may not have a bearing on the other. In a criminal case, the state is required to prove the guilt of the accused 'beyond a reasonable doubt'. This is not the same thing as 'beyond a shadow of doubt'. In this instance, the guilt of the accused must be overwhelming in such a way that any doubt that may still exist must be unreasonable.

In a civil case, the liability of the other party need only be proved on a 'balance of probabilities', i.e., just above 50 per cent. This means that a person who may not be proved guilty beyond a reasonable doubt may still be found liable on a balance of probabilities. Accordingly, the fact that a person has been found 'not guilty' in the criminal courts cannot itself be a basis for not pursuing civil action. However, it must be clear that a person found guilty beyond a reasonable doubt is clearly liable on a balance of probabilities.

The legislature has now stepped in to assist civil litigants where a person has already been found guilty in criminal courts. In terms of the Civil Evidence Act (Chapter 8:01), a conviction in a criminal court is admissible in a civil court. The Civil Evidence Act was enacted as Act Number 15/1992 and came into force on 15 October 1992. Section 31 (13) of the Act provides as follows:

> Where it is proved in any civil proceedings that a person has been convicted of a criminal offence, it shall be presumed unless the contrary is shown:
> a) That he did all acts necessary to constitute the offence; or
> b) Where the offence is constituted by omission to do anything, or that he omitted to do that thing, as the case may be.

Even where allegations of a criminal nature constitute the basis of a civil action, the standard of proof remains that of a balance of probabilities. A typical example is where an employee is accused of theft or fraud at the workplace and the employer institutes disciplinary proceedings with a view to terminating the contract of employment. In such disciplinary proceedings, the employer is only required to prove the theft or fraud on a balance of probabilities and, if successful, the employee may be dismissed. Should the employee be prosecuted, the state will have to prove the theft or fraud beyond a reasonable doubt. In *ZESA v Dera* the employee was accused of theft and the employer sought to dismiss him from employment.[1] A disciplinary committee found the employee guilty of theft on a balance of probabilities and authorized his dismissal. The employee subsequently appealed to the Labour Relations Tribunal, which reversed the disciplinary committee's ruling by holding that since the allegation was of a criminal nature, the employer had to prove it beyond any reasonable doubt. The employer successfully appealed to the Supreme Court, which rejected the approach of the Labour Relations Tribunal and reiterated that in all civil cases, including those where allegations are of a criminal nature, proof remains on a balance of probabilities. The Supreme Court also took the opportunity to state the rationale of the different standards of proof in criminal and civil cases. McNally JA said:

> It is a startling, and in my view, an entirely novel proposition, that in a civil case the standard of proof should be anything other than proof on a balance of probabilities. The reason, I have always understood, why in a criminal case proof beyond reasonable doubt is required, is that loss of a criminal case can result in death by hanging, incarceration, or at the least, the branding of a person as a criminal or convict. A criminal trial is an attack by the State, representing the whole of society, upon the integrity of an individual. Thus a person convicted of a crime is marked as one whose conduct stands condemned by society.
>
> A civil case, on the other hand, is merely a dispute between individuals. The loss of such a case, however ruinous in terms of money or property, loss of employment or loss of face, is not a judgment by society as a whole, but simply a resolution of the dispute between the parties.
>
> Moreover, parties in a civil dispute are equally interested parties, in the sense that each one seeks relief. X claims money from Y, Y claims an order that he owes nothing; X wishes to dismiss Y, Y wishes to remain employed. In a criminal matter the State does not stand to gain or lose by the outcome of the trial. So, if Y is acquitted of theft, the State does not suffer. But if X is forced to continue to employ Y, whom it has accused of theft, X does indeed suffer if Y, who is in fact a thief, is found 'not guilty'.
>
> In a criminal case one is primarily concerned with doing justice to the accused. In a civil case one is concerned to do justice to each party. Each party has a right to justice, and so the test for that justice has to balance their competing claims. Hence the 'balance of probability' test. ZESA, in the present case, has a right not to be forced to employ a thief; Dera has a right not to be dismissed unjustly. The law must balance those rights.[2]

To put this important distinction beyond doubt, the following passages from Gary Slapper and David Kelly's book, *The English Legal System*, are useful:

> Civil law is a form of private law and involves the relationship between individual citizens. It is the legal mechanism through which individuals can assert claims against others and have those rights adjudicated and enforced. The purpose of civil law is to settle disputes between individuals and to provide remedies; it is not concerned with punishment as such. The role of the state in relation to civil law is to establish the general framework of legal rules and to

provide the legal institutions to operate those rights, but the activation of the civil law is strictly a matter for the individuals concerned. Contract, tort and property law are generally aspects of civil law.

Criminal law, on the other hand, is an aspect of public law and relates to conduct which the state considers with disapproval and which it seeks to control and/or involves the *enforcement* of particular forms of behaviour, and the state, as the representative of society, acts positively to ensure compliance. Thus, criminal cases are brought by the state in the name of the Crown and cases are reported in the form of *Regina v* ... (Regina is simply Latin for 'queen' and case references are usually abbreviated to *R v* ...) whereas civil cases are referred to by the names of the parties involved in the dispute, for example *Smith v Jones*. In criminal law, a prosecutor prosecutes a defendant ('the accused'). In civil law, a claimant sues ('brings a claim against') a defendant.

In distinguishing between criminal and civil actions, it has to be remembered that the same event may give rise to both. For example, where the driver of a car injures someone through their reckless driving, they are liable for prosecution under the Road Traffic legislation. At the same time, they will also be responsible to the injured party in the civil law relating to the tort of negligence.[3]

Public law versus private law

Public law may be described as that law in which the state is a party to the relationship or the dispute, whereas private law regulates the rights and duties of persons among themselves. The state has direct matters over which it is involved in the day-to-day life of citizens. This is the province of public law.

Another way of expressing the distinction between public law and private law is to say that if one of the parties to the legal relationship is the state then it is public law and if it is not, it is private law.

Public law covers constitutional law, criminal law, law of taxation and administrative law. Here, the state is involved in its capacity as a sovereign power. Private law covers the law of property, of obligations (contract and delict) and of persons. The state may be regulated by private law where it is involved not as a sovereign power but as an ordinary person, such as where it enters into a contract to purchase goods and services.

In some cases, it is difficult to tell whether a particular law is public or private in nature. For example, with labour law, some aspects fall under public law, such as when workers seek to register a trade union, while others are clearly in the domain of private law, such as the relationship between the individual worker and the individual employer.

Substantive law versus procedural law

Substantive law deals with specific legal rights and duties of persons, such as the nature of the rights and duties, how these are constituted, how they are extinguished and their legal effect.

Procedural law is composed of rules that govern the enforcement of rights, i.e., the steps which should be taken to impose these rights. It is sometimes described as adjectival law and includes the law of criminal procedure, civil procedure and the law of evidence.

National law versus international law

National law refers to the body of rules peculiar to a particular country or state, while international law refers to rules that are binding on states in their relations with each other.

International law is sometimes described as public international law so as to distinguish it from private international law (conflict of laws). Private international law deals with the exercise of jurisdiction by national courts in matters involving a foreign element, such as jurisdiction over a foreigner or where the cause of action arose in a foreign state.

It has been argued that international law is not law because there is no supra-national body to enforce it. This argument is misplaced. Modern jurists regard it as law and the courts refer to it as such.[4] It is important to emphasize that the primary focus of international law is to regulate relations among states, not create rights for individual citizens. However, states may agree to create individual rights for their citizens and when this happens national law may be involved in the enforcement of those rights. An individual citizen has no right of audience before the International Court of Justice (ICJ).

In Zimbabwe, a rule of international law emanating from a treaty which has been ratified by Zimbabwe does not create legal rights for citizens under national law unless it has been incorporated into an Act of Parliament.[5] However, rules of customary international law are automatically regarded as part of our national law, except where they conflict with a statute or the common law.[6]

General law versus customary law

General law is made up of statute law and common law, whereas customary law refers to African customary law.

Customary law only applies to Africans as defined in the Interpretation Act (Chapter 1:01). Customs of Europeans in Zimbabwe do not constitute customary law. An 'African' is defined as 'any member of the aboriginal tribes or races of Africa and the islands adjacent thereto, including Madagascar and Zanzibar or any person who has the blood of such tribes or races and who lives as a member of an aboriginal native community.'

Common law versus civil law

A distinction is sometimes drawn between systems of law originating from Roman law (civil law systems) and those originating from English law (common law systems). The following passage from Smith and Bailey illustrates this distinction:

> The point that decisions of the superior courts are a source of law in their own right is a distinctive feature of 'common law systems', the term here being used to distinguish such systems from continental 'civil law' systems based in origin upon Roman Law but now upon a series of codes established in the nineteenth and twentieth centuries. The basic elements of English law have become established in a number of Commonwealth countries (most notably Australia, New Zealand and Canada, excluding Quebec) and the United States (except Louisiana).[7]

Law (common law) versus equity

Under English law, the common law is also distinguished from equity, a term which in popular usage refers to natural justice. In English law, equity has a technical meaning as that branch of law which is historically derived from justice administered by the Court of Chancery to alleviate the injustice stemming from the common law. In essence, the Court of Chancery was constituted by the Lord Chancellor, the King's Chief Minister, who dealt with petitions brought to the King by litigants who were dissatisfied with the common law.

By the end of the thirteenth century, the common law was being administered by three courts: the Exchequer, the Common Pleas and the King's (or Queen's) Bench. These courts applied the common law rigidly and this inevitably led to many situations of injustice. Many plaintiffs who could not obtain justice from the common law courts made direct appeals to the King, who passed them on to the Lord Chancellor. The Lord Chancellor, in these ad hoc interventions, acted as the King's conscience and decided matters on the basis of general principles of justice and common sense. These general principles of justice and common sense outside the common law came to be called *equity*. At one point it was said that the rules of equity 'varied according to the length of the Chancellor's foot'. However, with time, equity developed to be a body of principles also based on precedent and as rigid as the common law itself. Slapper and Kelly explain the development of equity in the following manner:

> Plaintiffs unable to gain access to the three common law courts might directly appeal to the sovereign, and such pleas would be passed for consideration and decision to the Lord Chancellor, who acted as the King's conscience. As the common law courts became more formalistic and more inaccessible, pleas to the Chancellor correspondingly increased and eventually this resulted in the emergence of a specific court constituted to deliver 'equitable' or 'fair' decisions in cases that the common law courts declined to deal with. As has happened with the common law, the decisions of the Courts of Equity established principles which were used to decide later cases; so it should not be thought that the use of equity meant that judges had discretion to decide cases on the basis of their personal idea of what was just in each case.[8]

Notes

1. 1998 (1) ZLR 500 (S).
2. Ibid., pp. 503-4.
3. Gary Slapper and David Kelly (2004) *The English Legal System*. Sixth edition, Cavendish Publishing: London, pp. 6-7.
4. See *In re Mashona* 1900 (17) SC 135, p. 152; *Baker v Government of Kenya*, 1983 (1) ZLR 137.
5. See 111(B) of the Constitution of Zimbabwe.
6. See *Barker v Government of Kenya*, 1983 (1) ZLR 137.
7. See Bailey and Gunn (1996), p.4.
8. See Slapper and Kelly (2004), p. 4.

4

The Law-Making Process

Introduction: State organs and their powers

The starting point to understanding state organs and their powers is to recall an oft-quoted statement from the opening paragraphs of the 1776 American Declaration of Independence:

> We hold these truths to be self evident, that all men are created equal, that they are endowed by their creator with certain inalienable rights, that among these are life, liberty and the pursuit of happiness. That to secure these rights, governments are instituted among men, deriving their just powers from the consent of the governed, that ... it is the right of the people ... to institute new government, laying its foundation on such principles, and organising its power in such form, as to them seem most likely to effect their safety and happiness.

This statement emphasizes the fact that the power of governmental organs is necessarily limited and defined by the society that creates the government. There is thus no magic in the powers of state organs; their power is given and defined by the people. Every society has rules that define the structures of the state and spell out their powers. These rules may be written or unwritten, or a combination of both. A totality of these rules make up what is called the *Constitution* of a country. The law emanating from such rules is called constitutional law. Professor Peter Hogg has aptly described constitutional law as follows:

> Constitutional law is the law prescribing the exercise of power by the organs of a state. It explains which organs can exercise legislative power (making new laws), executive power (implementing the laws) and judicial power (adjudicating disputes) and what the limitations of those powers are .... Civil liberties

are also part of constitutional law because civil liberties may be created by the rules that limit the exercise of governmental power over individuals.[1]

Indeed, in most countries, including Zimbabwe, the rules defining the structure and powers of governmental organs are embodied in its Constitution. It is mainly to these documented rules that reference should be made in order to understand the powers of state organs. Answers to the following questions are all a matter of constitutional law: Which organ(s) make(s) law? What are the requisite law-making processes?

Constitutional law utilizes the principle of *separation of powers*. In its classical sense, this principle of separation of powers requires that, as a guarantee for the liberty of the individual, political power should not be concentrated in one individual or organ of government. It requires that governmental functions be separated into three different groups and each be performed by different persons. This is thought to be a way of creating 'checks and balances' by one organ against another. The three main governmental organs are the legislature, the executive and the judiciary. Thus, the organ that makes law (the legislature) should be different from the organ which implements it (the executive) and should both be different from the organ which interprets it in the event of a dispute (the judiciary).

Although Zimbabwe has adopted the basic framework of creating three state organs in terms of the principle of separation of powers, it has not fully embraced the strict separation of functions of government into different organs and individuals. A brief description of the structure and functions of the key state organs is essential for an understanding of the law-making process.

The legislature (the law-makers)

A principal function of the state is that of making laws for the proper ordering of society. The popular conception of governance is that of making laws to be observed in and by the community. This important function of the state is allocated to the legislature, which in Zimbabwe consists of Parliament and the president.[2] Parliament itself is composed of two chambers: the House of Assembly (Lower House) and the Senate (Upper House).

For a law to be said to be a law made by the legislature in Zimbabwe, it must pass through two stages. First, it must be passed by the requisite majority in both houses of Parliament. Second, once it has been passed by Parliament, it should be assented to by the president before it becomes law.[3] This second stage makes the president very much part of the legislature in Zimbabwe. The president is a separate organ from Parliament, but he has the power to accept or reject laws that it has passed.[4] This is so, even though the president is also head of the executive, which implements the law. This state of affairs essentially allows the executive (the Cabinet) to have a final say on the law-making process.

The nature of this power relationship between the president and Parliament becomes particularly interesting when the former decides to reject a law duly passed by Parliament. Where this happens, the bill is returned to the House of Assembly, which then has two options: it can either agree with the president and drop the proposed law or it can send the bill back to the president. However, it can only send the bill back if it has resolved to do so by a two-thirds majority. A simple majority is not enough to disagree with the president. On being presented with the bill for a second time, the president then has two options: assent to the proposed law or dissolve Parliament and call for fresh elections.[5] This shows that while Parliament has the power to force the president into signing a law, this power is limited because the latter may override it by dissolution.

Before the 2007 Constitution of Zimbabwe Amendment No. 18, the House of Assembly was composed of 150 members, 120 of whom were elected by the people of Zimbabwe in 120 constituencies. The remaining 30 comprised 12 Presidential appointees; ten Provincial Governors – ex-officio members of Parliament appointed by the president; and eight traditional chiefs elected by chiefs in electoral colleges constituted in terms of Section 40 of the Electoral Act (Chapter 2:01).[6] Today, the House of Assembly is composed of 210 members, all of whom are directly elected.

Before Amendment 18, the Senate was composed of 66 members, 50 of whom were elected by the people of Zimbabwe in 50 senatorial constituencies. The remaining 16 comprised the president and Deputy president of the Council of Chiefs; eight chiefs, elected by chiefs in terms of the Electoral Law and representing each of the eight provinces which are not metropolitan provinces; and six Presidential appointees. Today, the Senate is composed of 93 members, 60 of whom are elected in 60 senatorial constituencies. The other 33 comprise the president and Deputy president of the Council of Chiefs; 16 chiefs – two from each of the eight rural provinces; ten provincial governors; and five Presidential appointees.

The House of Assembly is presided over by the Speaker, who is elected by members at their first sitting. He/she cannot vote in the passing of laws. Even a person who is not a member of the House of Assembly may be elected a Speaker, provided he/she has been a member of Parliament before and meets the qualifications for election to the House of Assembly. However, only a member of the House of Assembly qualifies to be elected Deputy Speaker.[7] If a member of the House of Assembly is elected Speaker, he/she shall cease to be a member and his/her seat shall become vacant and a by-election called.

The Senate is presided over by the president of the Senate, who is also elected by members at their first sitting. As with the House of Assembly, even a person who is not a member of the Senate may be elected as president of the Senate, provided he/she has been a member of Parliament before and meets the qualifications for election to the Senate. If a Senator is elected as president of the Senate, he/she shall cease to be a Senator and his/her seat shall become vacant and a by-election called.

Apart from its law-making functions, Parliament also has the power to supervise the executive arm of government by, among other things, criticizing government policies. Through this role, Parliament has the power to institute investigations into any activity of the state and to publicize its findings. This power can be used to ensure accountability on the part of government ministers. The most important manifestation of this power is the 'question and answer' session in Parliament, where parliamentarians are entitled to ask government ministers any questions pertaining to the conduct of government and the latter are obliged to answer those questions truthfully. The answers given in Parliament are essentially for the benefit of the public. Members of the public seeking answers to questions of public importance may do so by asking their MPs to pose the relevant question(s) in Parliament. In Zimbabwe, fear of facing embarrassing questions in Parliament may 'force' government ministers to maintain some respect for the law and the rights of the people.

The executive

The executive arm of government is composed of the president, the Cabinet, and all law enforcement agencies of the state, namely, the police, the military and the prison service.[8] The ultimate authority of the executive functions of the state is vested in the president, who exercises most of his functions through the Cabinet.

The president is elected for a five-year term by all registered voters. There is currently no limit to the number of terms a person may serve as president of Zimbabwe.[9] He/she has sole power to appoint and dismiss Vice Presidents and Ministers; to dissolve Parliament; and to appoint Provincial Governors.[10] He/she has to act on the advice of the Cabinet to appoint ambassadors, to enter into international treaties, to proclaim martial law and to declare war. The president's exercise of his/her discretion – 'deliberate judgement' – in performing tasks permitted by the Constitution cannot be questioned in a court of law.[11]

The role of the executive arm of government is to implement laws made by Parliament and to run the affairs of the state. The executive also has the responsibility to initiate policy, and in that regard it is empowered to propose laws for consideration by Parliament. Although the theory of separation of powers in its absolute sense would require that members of Parliament be separate from members of the executive, the system in Zimbabwe requires members of the executive to be drawn from Parliament. If the president appoints a minister from outside Parliament, that person must obtain a seat in Parliament within three months or the appointment will lapse.

The judiciary

The judiciary is an arm of the state. However, judges are required to be independent in the discharge of their duties.[12] This independence of the judiciary from the other two arms of the state is the cornerstone of the theory of 'separation of powers'. The function of the judiciary is to interpret the law, something that the two other organs cannot do. If the executive and/or the legislature is/are not happy with a certain interpretation of the law by the courts, the only way out is to seek a change to the law rather than disregard the interpretation and argue that it is wrong. The prerogative to interpret the law lies only with the judiciary.

One of the most important functions of the judiciary in Zimbabwe is that of adjudicating on the constitutionality of Acts of Parliament. An Act of Parliament or any other law which contravenes the Constitution can be declared unlawful by the Supreme Court.[13] This power has already been exercised in a number of well-known cases. These include:

a) The suspension of Mr Ian Douglas Smith's salary after he had been suspended from Parliament was held to be unlawful because it

THE LAW-MAKING PROCESS

contravened Section 16 of the Constitution, which prohibits compulsory acquisition of property without adequate compensation.[14]

b) The requirement in the old Law and Order Maintenance Act that police permission be sought before holding a public meeting was held to be unlawful because it contravened Section 21, which protects freedom of assembly.[15]

c) Corporal punishment was declared unlawful because it contravened Section 15, which protects human dignity.[16]

d) The compulsory requirement that a national ID be carried at all times was declared unlawful as it contravened Section 22 of the Constitution, which protects freedom of movement.[17]

e) The monopoly of the Posts and Telecommunications Corporation was declared unlawful as a contravention of the freedom of expression protected by Section 20.[18]

This power of the Supreme Court to determine the constitutionality of Acts of Parliament puts an independent judiciary in a secure position to exert checks and balances on the powers of the executive and the legislature. However, by a proper amendment of laws, Parliament can nullify certain decisions of the courts.

The Supreme Court is headed by the Chief Justice. To maintain judges' independence, the Constitution has a number of measures in place, and these are discussed in Chapter 6.

Other key organs

The division of government organs into three main groups can mask certain bodies that require separate treatment, the most important of which are the Offices of the Attorney General, the Comptroller and Auditor-General, and the Public Protector.

The Attorney General

The Attorney General is another important organ of the state.[19] He/she has two main functions, namely, (i) being the chief legal adviser to the Government and (ii) prosecuting criminal offences. As legal adviser to the Government, he/she sits, without voting rights, in both the Cabinet and Parliament. He/she represents all government departments in all actions that may be brought against them in court.

In prosecuting criminal offences, the Attorney General is required to act without fear or favour and to decide or decline to prosecute without pressure from any political leaders. He/she is entitled to order the prosecution of criminal offences even where they have been committed by very senior members of the Government. The Attorney General also has the power to ask the Commissioner of Police to investigate suspected offences and the latter is obliged to follow his/her request(s).

The Comptroller & Auditor-General

The Comptroller and Auditor-General is a public officer appointed by the president to examine and audit all government accounts at least once every year.[20] He/she is required to report to Parliament all his/her findings and to be completely independent in the discharge of his/her duties. Once reported to Parliament, these accounts become available to members of the public. The report of the Comptroller and Auditor-General is a useful source of information for members of the public to use for purposes of criticizing government's approaches to its finances.

The Public Protector

Before Constitution of Zimbabwe Amendment 18 of 2007, this office was known as 'The Ombudsman'. The Public Protector is appointed by the president for the purpose of investigating any complaints of members of the public against government departments and statutory corporations.[21] The office of the Public Protector is a public office and therefore available for use by all people in Zimbabwe.

The process of law-making in Parliament

The Constitution of Zimbabwe specifies the manner in which Parliament legislates. Section 51 provides that 'the power of Parliament to make laws shall be exercised by bills passed by the House of Assembly and the Senate and assented to by the president'. This means that Parliament can only make law through the passing of bills. Schedule 4 of the Constitution sets out some, but not all, aspects of the procedures involved. The Constitution empowers Parliament to make what are called 'Standing Orders' which prescribe the procedure for the passing of bills.[22] Accordingly, the two sources to which reference must be made in terms of the procedure for the passing of bills are (i) Schedule 4 of the Constitution and (ii) Standing Orders of Parliament. Standing Orders constitute a special form of legislation that is sanctioned by the Constitution. If Parliament attempts to pass bills contrary to the procedure set out in the Standing Orders, the resultant Act is invalid and of no force or effect.[23]

Pre-bill stage

This is the stage leading to the finalization of the proposals that are contained in the bill that is sent to Parliament. This is exclusively a political process dominated by the executive. Legislative proposals result from a variety of sources such as political party manifestos, government departments, commissions of enquiry, parliamentary portfolio committees, pressure groups and responses to disasters.

A major issue is the extent to which government is obliged to consult interested parties before presenting a bill to Parliament. There is no legal obligation under the laws of Zimbabwe for the Government to consult, let alone to be bound by the views of, any person before presenting a bill to Parliament. Consultations are carried out at the Government's discretion. In other systems, this is not the case. Some countries have constitutionally entrenched legal requirements for the executive to consult and to state, in a memorandum to Parliament, what steps have been taken to solicit the views of the people.

In the United Kingdom, the practice is to issue either a 'white paper' or a 'green paper' before sending bills to Parliament. A white paper states proposals without government expressing a view and calling for public discussion, whereas a green paper sets out tentative proposals of government and calls for comments on them. After discussions, a bill is then formulated, purportedly taking into account the inputs of the public discussion.

The process of how proposals eventually become bills is largely shrouded in secrecy, but appears to be as follows:

1. Cabinet makes a policy decision that a certain law is to be made, for example, to restrict the media or ban foreign funding of NGOs.
2. The decision is communicated to the relevant government department by the relevant ministers. It must in turn prepare a set of detailed principles to govern the legislation.
3. These principles are sent to the Cabinet Committee on Legislation (CCL). This is a sub-committee of cabinet tasked with supervising legislative

drafting. Its function is to debate and approve the principles in the light of the policy spelt out by the full cabinet.

4. From the CCL, the principles are sent to the Attorney General's office, where a drafts person is appointed and assigned the role of drafting the piece of legislation. He/she must work in constant consultation with the relevant government department.

5. When the department is satisfied with the draft, it sends a draft bill together with an accompanying memorandum to the CCL, which must scrutinize it in the light of the principles and the policy articulated by the full cabinet.

6. After approval by the CCL, the bill may either be sent to the full cabinet, in case of important or controversial bills, or to Parliament, if the CCL has been mandated to follow that route.

Types of bills

A distinction must be drawn between public and private bills. Public bills are those that are intended to alter the general law or to deal with public revenue or the administration of justice. Private bills deal with matters of a private or local nature such as legislation promoted by local authorities or relating to the property of private individuals. Within the class of public bills, a further distinction is drawn between a government bill (introduced by a government minister) and a private member's bill (introduced by an individual Member of Parliament).

Gazetting of bills

The *Government Gazette* is the official publication of the Government of Zimbabwe. It is the legal medium through which the Government informs the public about its legal instruments. Except for constitutional bills, the Constitution does not require that a bill be gazetted before it is introduced in Parliament. A constitutional bill is one that seeks to amend or repeal any of the provisions of the Constitution. The text of such a bill must be published in the *Government Gazette* not less than 30 days before it is introduced in Parliament.[24] For all other bills, the Standing Orders require that they be published in the gazette at least 14 days before being introduced in Parliament.[25] This requirement, however, may be waived and the bill introduced without being gazetted 'in cases of urgency' upon the application of a Vice president or Minister.

Passage of bills in Parliament

As Parliament has two houses, a bill must be introduced in and passed by both to become law. The same stages are followed by each house. In general, the process in one house must be completed before the bill is introduced in the second house. Except for a type of bill known as a 'Money Bill', which may only originate in the House of Assembly, a bill may originate in either house.[26] A Money Bill (defined in Section 6(9) of Schedule 4 of the Constitution) is a public bill which provides for all or any of the following matters: imposition or administration of taxation, the imposition of charges on the Consolidated Revenue Fund; the making or raising of any loan by the government, and the condoning of unauthorized expenditure.

Stage 1 – First reading

After a bill has been gazetted, the member responsible must serve notice of a motion that leave be granted by the House to bring in the bill. On the day specified in the notice, the motion for leave is moved and, if granted, the member must bring a copy of the bill to the clerks at the table, who read the title of the bill. It is the bringing of the copy to the clerks and the subsequent reading of the title thereof which is regarded as the first reading.

Stage 2 – Reference to the Parliamentary Legal Committee (PLC)

The house in which the bill originates refers it to the Parliamentary Legal Committee (PLC). This committee is set up in terms of Section 40A of the Constitution and its functions are spelt out in Section 40B. Its purpose is to examine all bills and statutory instruments and determine whether or not they are in conformity with the Bill of Rights and any other provisions of the Constitution. If the committee makes an adverse report, i.e., finding that the provisions of the bill contravene the Bill of Rights and/or some Sections of the Constitution, it is referred to the House of Assembly or the Senate, as the case may be. It would appear that the House of Assembly has the power to reject the opinion of the Parliamentary Legal Committee.[27] If it does reject the opinion, it will proceed with the bill as if no adverse report were given. If, on the other hand, it agrees with the report, the bill will not be passed.[28] If the Parliamentary Legal Committee fails to present its report within the period specified in the Standing Orders, it shall be presumed that there is no adverse report and the House of Assembly shall proceed with the bill.

Stage 3 – Second reading

This third stage is opened by the sponsoring minister, who makes a speech outlining the purpose of the bill and the principles upon which it is based. This is followed by debate on these principles. No discussion on individual clauses is permissible, although reference may be made to these clauses as part of the debate. In some western democracies, a government that loses a bill at this stage may be forced to resign. Following recent reforms to Zimbabwe's parliamentary system, it is at this stage that the relevant Parliamentary Portfolio Committee (PPC) will present its report on the bill. PPCs are appointed for every government department and one of their functions is to scrutinize proposed bills, which includes conducting public hearings and presenting a report to Parliament. It is expected that the chairperson of the PPC will contribute to the debate on principles based on the committee's findings.

Stage 4 – Consideration by committee

Next, the bill is considered clause by clause, either by a special committee set up for the purpose or a committee of the whole house. The practice in Zimbabwe is to use a committee of the whole house. At this stage, amendments to individual clauses are proposed and debated. Amendments are not usually successful if they run against the wishes of the Government. The committee stage is chaired by the Deputy Speaker or Deputy president, as the case may be, and he/she is addressed as chairperson. Amendments proposed by the PPC are also discussed at this stage.

Stage 5 – Reporting

This stage involves making a report of the bill, as amended, to the whole house. If the bill was considered by a committee of the whole house, the report stage is a mere formality. If it was considered by a special committee, this stage allows other members of the house to propose amendments. Government may also use this stage to reverse amendments made at committee stage or to add new clauses arising from any subsequent deliberations.

Stage 6 – Referall to the PLC

If the bill is amended at the committee and/or report stages, it is referred to the PLC, which will scrutinize any amendments according to the procedures outlined in Stage 2.

THE LAW-MAKING PROCESS

Stage 7 – Third reading

This is the stage at which the bill is put to a vote for either approval or rejection. No reading per se takes place and, unless some members have given notice that they wish to do so, there is no debate. The quorum, i.e., the minimum number of people required to constitute a valid meeting of the House of Assembly is 25 members. For the Senate it is 11.[29] For an ordinary bill to pass, there must be a majority from those present and voting. However, for a Constitutional Bill to pass, there must be at least a two-thirds majority from the total membership of each house.

Stage 8 – Transmission to the other house

As soon as the bill has been passed by the house in which it originated, an authenticated copy of it is transmitted to the other house. The second house may reject the bill or pass it with or without amendments. Where the second house passes the bill with amendments, it returns the bill to the house of origin. The house of origin may reject, agree to, or incorporate the amendments made to the bill by the second house.[30] Disagreements between the two houses are dealt with in the manner provided for in paragraph 3 of Schedule 4. However, primacy is given to the House of Assembly in the following ways:

- If a bill originates in the Senate and is totally rejected by the House of Assembly, that is the end of the bill.
- If a bill originates in the House of Assembly and is totally rejected by the Senate, the House of Assembly may still present the bill to the President for assent in its existing form, except for minor changes required by the passage of time. However, the House of Assembly can only present the bill to the President after the expiration of 90 days from the day of the introduction of the bill to the Senate and after passing a resolution to that effect.
- Where a disagreement relates to amendments made to a bill, the House of Assembly may present the bill to the President for assent in the form in which it was passed, i.e., including any amendments it may have agreed with the Senate. However, this may only be done after the expiration of 90 days beginning on: a) the day of the introduction of the bill into the Senate (if the bill originated in the House of Assembly) or (b) the day of the return of the bill to the Senate (if the bill originated in the Senate). Again, a resolution to that effect is required.
- If a bill originates in the House of Assembly and the Senate, although

not rejecting the bill, has not passed it before the expiration of 90 days from the day of its introduction into the Senate, the House of Assembly may still present the bill to the President as in (ii) above. In other words, if the Senate delays in passing a bill, it may be overridden by the House of Assembly.

- A Vice President or a Minister may certify that a bill (other than a constitutional bill) originating in the House of Assembly and passed by that house is so urgent that it is not in the national interest to delay its enactment. Such a bill may be presented to the President for his/her assent in the form in which it was passed by the House of Assembly after the expiration of eight sitting days beginning on the day of its introduction into the Senate, if there is no agreement between the two houses on amendments to be made, or if the Senate has not passed the bill within that period.

When a bill has been returned by the second house to the house in which it originated, the latter shall consider the amendments made by the other house and make a resolution on whether or not it agrees to them. It shall then communicate its resolution to the other house by a 'message'.[31]

Stage 9 – Presidential assent

A bill becomes law only after being assented to by the president. After a bill has been passed by both houses, or after the House of Assembly has overridden the Senate, it is presented to the president for assent. In the case of a constitutional bill, it must be accompanied by certificates from the Speaker and the president of the Senate certifying that it was approved by the requisite two-thirds majority.[32] As already discussed, the president is not obliged to assent to a bill; he/she has unlimited discretion in this regard. Again, if the president rejects the bill in question, but the House of Assembly subsequently secures the relevant two-thirds majority and returns the bill to the president, he/she is given two options: either assent to the bill within 21 days or dissolve Parliament and call for fresh elections.

The effect of Parliament's failure to follow specified procedures

Should Parliament attempt to pass a bill contrary to the procedures examined above, the law is that the resultant Act is invalid and the courts are empowered to intervene and declare the Act of no force or effect. *Biti and the MDC v Minister of Justice Legal and Parliamentary Affairs* provides a good example.[33] Here the applicants challenged the General Laws Amendment Act (Act No. 2 of 2002) and sought to have it declared illegal and of no force or effect as it had introduced far-reaching and controversial changes to the Electoral Act ahead of the 2002 Presidential elections.

These purported amendments were viewed by the applicants as favouring the ruling party and seriously prejudicing the opposition. The relevant bill had gone through the usual parliamentary procedures up until the third reading. However, when a vote was taken on the motion for the third reading, Government received an unexpected defeat by 36 votes to 24, which effectively killed the bill. True to its undemocratic instincts, the Government nevertheless refused to accept defeat. The following day, the Minister of Justice gave notice that he would move a motion that Parliament rescind its decision on the third reading. The rescission was to be in terms of Order 69. He also gave notice that he would move to suspend the provisions of Order 127, which provides that no bill shall be reintroduced in Parliament during the same session in which it had been negated. The very next day, the two motions were moved and passed by Parliament. A new third reading was then approved by a vote of 62 to 49. This meant that the bill was now considered passed by Parliament. The president subsequently assented to the bill and the Act was promulgated on 4 February 2002, in time for the Presidential election. The contention of the applicants was that Parliament had failed to follow the correct legal procedures, in that it had breached the Constitution and the Standing Orders. The bill had therefore not been properly passed and the Act was invalid, it was argued.

These contentions were accepted by the Supreme Court in a four-to-one ruling and the Act was nullified. Ebrahim JA, who presided over the full bench in the absence of Chief Justice Chidyausiku, wrote the majority opinion. He had a two-pronged reasoning: first he held that Order 69, which gave Parliament some powers of rescission of motions, did not apply to the passing of bills, but only to motions, and therefore did not authorize the procedure adopted by the Minister of Justice. Second, even assuming that Parliament could suspend Order 127 and allow the reintroduction of a second bill in the same session, that second bill had to be introduced in accordance with the normal procedures and not by starting at the stage at which the bill had been negated. As the Minister had gone straight into a new third reading without starting afresh, this was held improper and unlawful.

Malaba JA dissented from the view of the majority. He reasoned that the vote taken after the third reading was irrelevant and purported to base this on Order 124. That order provides that after the third reading no further questions shall be put and the bill shall be deemed to have been passed by Parliament. He said:

> My interpretation of Order 124 is that the question put to the house on the passage of the bill after it had been read for the third time was not legally permissible. By the time that question was raised, the bill had passed and the majority vote could not affect the passage of the bill. The vote was in fact null and void.[34]

This attempt to separate the third reading from the vote taken to approve it is fallacious. A bill is only said to have been 'read' after an affirmative vote has been taken to approve the reading.

Delegated legislation

Parliament may delegate its law-making powers to a variety of public authorities, particularly the president, Ministers and Local Authorities. Legislation emanating from these authorities in exercise of the powers granted to them by Parliament is called 'delegated legislation'. The extent of the power to make law in this way is regulated in each case by the relevant Act of Parliament (the 'enabling Act' or 'parent Act'). Section 32 (2) of the Constitution of Zimbabwe allows Parliament to delegate its law-making powers. It makes it clear that the legislature is empowered to confer legislative functions on any person or authority. The system of delegated legislation is subject to two controls, namely:

1. Delegated legislation, like any other legislation, must be consistent with the Constitution, i.e., it must be *intra vires* the Constitution.
2. It must be consistent with the parent Act, i.e., not *ultra vires* the enabling Act.

In some cases, there are procedural safeguards in the enactment of delegated legislation. Some statutes require the statutory instruments to be laid before Parliament. For example, the Presidential Powers (Temporary Measures) Act (Chapter 10:20) states that legislation made by the president must be laid before Parliament no more than eight sitting days after it has been promulgated.[35] The Act goes further in Section 4 (2) to give Parliament the power to amend this legislation.

Under the Constitution, the Parliamentary Legal Committee (PLC) is required to examine every statutory instrument published in the *Gazette* with a view to determining if it is consistent with the Constitution.[36]

If it presents an adverse report on a statutory instrument, the report is presented to both houses but it is the duty of the Senate to consider the report. If the Senate resolves to accept the PLC's opinion, the clerk of Parliament shall report to the president, who shall repeal the provision forthwith. Any such resolution must be made within 21 sitting days after the Senate resolves to accept an adverse opinion of the PLC.

The system of delegated legislation has been criticized for giving the executive too much power, something that is contrary to the principle of separation of powers. In the absence of effective safeguards, delegated legislation may be an avenue of undermining the fundamental rights of persons. An example of an overly wide provision is contained in the former Electoral Act (Chapter 2:01). Section 158 provided that:

> Notwithstanding any other provision of this Act, but subject to sub-Section 2, the President may make such statutory instruments as he considers necessary or desirable to ensure that any election is properly and efficiently conducted, and to deal with any matter or situation connected with, arising out of or resulting from the election.

The statutory instruments made in terms of sub-Section 1 may provide for:

> [S]uspending or amending any provision of this Act or any other law in so far as it applies to any election.
>
> [A]ltering any period specified in this Act within anything connected with, arising out of or resulting from any election must be done.
>
> [V]alidating anything done in connection with, arising out of or resulting from any election in contravention of any provision of this Act or any other law.

The president routinely resorted to this Section. In the run-up to the 2002 Presidential elections, President Mugabe promulgated a statutory instrument that modified the provisions of the Act relating to postal votes, taking away the right to a postal vote from all persons except members of security forces.

In the same statutory instrument, he barred white Zimbabweans who had purportedly lost their citizenship from voting. Morgan Tsvangirai, the leader of the opposition, rushed to the Supreme Court to challenge Section 158, arguing that it was unconstitutional. Chidyausiku CJ dismissed the application on the basis that Tsvangirai had no *locus standi*.[37]

After the 2000 Parliamentary elections, the MDC filed 37 petitions challenging results in 37 constituencies.

THE LAW-MAKING PROCESS

The president promulgated a statutory instrument nullifying electoral petitions, arguing that they were influenced by foreign forces and were straining the time and resources of the sitting MPs whose seats were being challenged. The MDC challenged this statutory instrument in the Supreme Court and Gubbay CJ upheld the application and set aside the statutory instrument on the basis that it infringed the right of access to the courts as entrenched in the Constitution.[38]

This notwithstanding, the system of delegated legislation may be defended on the following grounds:

- Pressure on parliamentary time – if all legislation were passed by Parliament, it would be in continuous session.
- The technicality of the subject matter of particular legislation, for example, the statutory instrument on hazardous drugs. In such areas, it makes sense to leave legislation to the experts.
- The difficulty of working out all necessary administrative details before a bill is presented to Parliament.
- The need to maintain flexibility so that legislation can be easily adapted to unknown future conditions without needing to seek approval for such amendments, for example, the prescription of interest rates.
- The need, from time to time, to deal with an emergency situation.

Notes

1. See Peter W. Hogg (2006) *Constitutional Law of Canada*. Toronto : Carswell Legal Publications, p. 1.
2. See Section 32 (1) of the Constitution of Zimbabwe.
3. Ibid., see Section 51 (1).
4. Ibid., Section 51 (2).
5. Ibid., Sections 51 (3a) and (3b).
6. Ibid., Section 38 (1).
7. Ibid., Section 39.
8. Ibid., Sections 27 and 31 H.
9. Ibid., Section 29. Before the Constitution of Zimbabwe Amendment 18 of 2007, the President's term of office was six years.
10. Ibid., Sections 31c, 31d and 31h, respectively.
11. Ibid., Section 31k.
12. Ibid., Section 79.
13. See Section 3 of the Constitution of Zimbabwe as read with Section 24.
14. *Smith v Mutasa* 2989 (3) ZLR 183.
15. *In re Munhumeso* 1994 (1) ZLR 49 (S).

16. *S v Ncube Ors* 1987 (2) ZLR.
17. *Elliot v Commissioner of Police & Anor* 1997 (1) ZLR 315 (S).
18. *Refrofit (Pvt) Ltd v Minister of Information* 1995 (2) ZLR 422 (S). This paved the way for the provision of cellular telephones by other players.
19. See Section 76 of the Constitution of Zimbabwe.
20. Ibid., Section 105.
21. Ibid., Sections 107 and 108.
22. Ibid., Section 57.
23. See *Tendai Biti and MDC v Justice, Legal and Parliamentary Affairs and the Attorney General*, 2002(1) ZLR 177(S).
24. See Section 52 (2) of the Constitution of Zimbabwe.
25. See Standing Order 102.
26. See Schedule 4, Section 1 (2) of the Constitution of Zimbabwe.
27. Ibid., paragraph 4 (3) of Schedule 4.
28. Ibid.
29. Ibid., Section 54.
30. See paragraph 2 of Schedule 4.
31. Ibid., paragraph 7.
32. See Section 52 (5) of the Constitution of Zimbabwe.
33. 2002 (1) ZLR 177.
34. Ibid., p. 195.
35. See Section 4 of the Act.
36. See Section 40B of the Constitution of Zimbabwe.
37. See *Tsvangirai and Others v Registrar General* 2002 (1) ZLR 268 (S).
38. See *Shepherd Mushonga and the MDC v Patrick Chinamasa, Minister of Justice* 2001 (1) ZLR 69 (S).

5

The Structure of the Courts

The Division between Criminal Courts & Civil Courts

Courts are classified into two broad categories, namely, *criminal courts* and *civil courts*. Civil courts in turn are divided into two groups: ordinary civil courts and specialized courts. In examining each court, two questions arise, namely, what is its composition? and what is its jurisdiction? To answer both, reference must be made to the Constitution of Zimbabwe and the relevant Act of Parliament regulating the operations of the court in question. In Zimbabwe, there is specific legislation that prescribes the composition and jurisdiction of each court.

The composition of a court refers to its judicial officers, i.e., whether a judge or a magistrate presides; the number of presiding judicial officers required to constitute the court; the qualifications the presiding officers must have; whether there is provision for assessors; and if so, the manner in which they are selected. The jurisdiction of the court refers to its powers and the matters over which it has competence and also determines its position in the structure of the courts, particularly how it relates to other courts.

Criminal Courts

There are three main criminal courts in Zimbabwe, namely, the Magistrates Court, the High Court and the Supreme Court. Five other 'courts' exercise specialized criminal jurisdiction. These are Children's Courts,

Courts-Martial, Police Boards of Officers, Prison Boards of Officers and Parliament sitting as a court in matters involving breach of parliamentary privileges.

Magistrates Court

This is the lowest criminal court in Zimbabwe. Two pieces of legislation govern its operations. These are the Magistrates Court Act (Chapter 7:10) and the Criminal Procedure and Evidence Act (Chapter 9:07).

Composition

A Magistrates Court is presided over by a magistrate.[1] In criminal matters, magistrates can be divided into four classes: ordinary magistrates, senior magistrates, provincial magistrates and regional magistrates. A Magistrates Court may be presided over by any of these four. In theory, there is no minimum qualification for a person to be appointed as an ordinary magistrate – any 'fit and proper person' may be so appointed. In practice, however, only persons who have undergone some legal training are appointed as magistrates.

The Magistrates Court Act itself specifies minimum qualifications for appointment to the other classes of magistrates. Ordinary magistrates who have held office for four years or more, or those who have been qualified to practice as legal practitioners for no less than four years, may be appointed as senior magistrates. Provincial magistrates are appointed from the ranks of senior magistrates. Regional magistrates are normally appointed from the ranks of provincial magistrates.

In a criminal trial, a magistrate may either sit alone or preside with the assistance of one or two assessors.[2] The circumstances under which an assessor or assessors may be appointed depend on whether the court is being presided over by a regional magistrate or by a lesser magistrate. For a regional magistrate, the decision whether or not to have an assessor lies with him/her but is still subject to the directions of the chief magistrate. It is the regional magistrate who decides whether to have one or two assessors. However, he/she must choose the assessor or assessors from persons who are qualified in terms of Section 6 of the High Court Act (Chapter 7:06) to act as assessors in the High Court. For any other magistrate, the decision whether or not to sit with an assessor or assessors requires the approval of the Minister of Justice.[3] The Minister must also approve the choices of assessors, who in this case, need not be qualified to act as assessors in the High Court but merely be persons who have 'experience in the administration of justice or skill in any matter which may have to be considered at the trial'.[4]

The role of assessors is limited to matters of fact. Any matter of law arising for decision at the trial is decided by the magistrate and assessors have no say over such a decision. In matters of fact and where there are two assessors, each has an equal voice with the magistrate and the finding of the court is that reached by the majority. Where there is one assessor, it is the decision of the magistrate that counts if there is a difference of opinion.[5] The fixing of a sentence is the sole responsibility of the magistrate although he/she may consult the assessor or assessors if he/she thinks it necessary to do so.[6]

Jurisdiction

The jurisdiction of a Magistrates Court is determined by three aspects; the territory where the crime takes place; the nature of the crime and the punishment that may be imposed. Regarding territory, a Magistrates Court has no jurisdiction over common law crimes committed outside Zimbabwe. In technical terms, it is said that the court has no extra-territorial jurisdiction over a common law crime. However, it has extra-territorial jurisdiction over a statutory crime where the statute in question has extra-territorial effect.[7] For crimes committed in Zimbabwe, the general rule is that a Magistrates Court only has jurisdiction over offences occurring in the region or province in which it is established. In this regard, Section 56 (1) of the Magistrates Court Act provides as follows:

> Subject to sub-Section (1) of Section forty-nine, any person charged with any offence committed within any province or regional division may be tried by the court of that province or that regional division, as the case may be.

Exceptions to this general rule include: (i) a court may have jurisdiction for an offence committed within five kilometres beyond its boundary, (ii) where any element of the offence takes place in a given province or region, the court therein may have jurisdiction even though the other elements of the offence have taken place outside the province or region and (iii) the Attorney General, with the consent of the accused, may direct that the trial be held in the court of any province.[8]

A Magistrates Court has jurisdiction over all crimes except treason, murder and any statutory offence for which the death sentence is mandatory.[9] However, not every Magistrates Court has jurisdiction to try rape cases. Only regional magistrates have jurisdiction to try cases of rape, except where the Attorney General has authorized trial or sentencing before a magistrate who is not a regional magistrate.[10]

The jurisdiction of Magistrates Courts regarding possible punishment depends on the level of the magistrate presiding over the court. The general power of an ordinary magistrate is limited to handing down sentences of imprisonment not exceeding 12 months. However, this increases to two years for a matter remitted by the Attorney General under 'increased jurisdiction' and to five years under 'special jurisdiction' for the common law crimes of public violence, arson and malicious injury to property.[11] For a senior magistrate, sentencing in a trial or matter remitted by the Attorney General is limited to a term of imprisonment not exceeding two years, while a provincial magistrate may hand down a maximum sentence of three years. Both a senior magistrate and provincial magistrate may also exercise 'special jurisdiction' over the common law offences of arson, public violence and malicious injury to property, for which maximum sentencing is five years. The general jurisdiction of a regional magistrate is limited to maximum sentencing of seven years, but this increases to ten years on a special jurisdiction over the offences of rape, public violence, arson, malicious injury to property and robbery (where aggravating circumstances are found to be present).

The High Court

The relevant pieces of legislation regulating the composition and jurisdiction of the High Court are the Constitution of Zimbabwe and the High Court Act.[12]

Composition

Under Section 81 (3) of the Constitution, the High Court consists of the Chief Justice, the Judge-president of the High Court, and such other judges as may be appointed. The qualifications for appointment as a judge of the High Court are set out in Section 82 of the Constitution (see chapter 6). In a criminal trial, the High Court is considered duly constituted if composed of one judge and two assessors.[13] When reviewing any criminal proceedings of an inferior court, one or more judges are required, while in an appeal it is mandatory that it be constituted by at least two judges.[14] Assessors are not required in reviews and appeals.

Section 6 (1) of the High Court Act sets out the qualifications for an assessor. He/she must be a person with experience in the administration of justice or have experience or skill in any matter to be considered at the trial. In the case of the trial of a juvenile, he/she must have experience or skill in dealing with juveniles or 'any other experience or qualification which, in the opinion of the Chief Justice and the Judge-president renders him suitable to act as an assessor in a criminal trial'.[15] The Minister of Justice prepares the list of assessors and the list must be approved by the Chief Justice and the Judge-president.[16] The choice of the two assessors for a particular trial is made from the list by the Registrar of the High Court.[17] However, the Chief Justice or the Judge-president may direct the Registrar as to the manner of choosing assessors from the list.

The function of assessors is to decide questions of fact. They do this together with the judge. The decision of the court on matters of fact is reached by majority. Thus, where the two assessors reach a conclusion different from that of the judge, their view prevails.[18] The judge alone decides on questions of law, including the decision as to whether a question is one of fact or of law. It is the responsibility of the judge to give reasons for the decisions of the court, including those where he/she is in the minority on questions of fact. Where there is a difference of opinion on a question of fact, the judge must give reasons for the finding of the dissenting member, even where that member is an assessor.[19]

It is not uncommon for judges to disagree. Section 4 of the High Court Act provides, in detail, what should happen in the event of a difference of opinion:

1. When more than two judges of the High Court are sitting together, the decision of the majority shall be the decision of the High Court.

2. Whenever there is a difference of opinion on an appeal or application or any other matter being heard by an even number of judges of the High Court sitting together and the opinions are equally divided, the decision of the High Court shall be suspended until the opinion of a further judge of the High Court has been obtained, and thereupon the decision of the majority of such judges shall be the decision of the High Court.

3. If at any stage during the hearing of an appeal or application or any other matter by three or more judges of the High Court any such judge dies or retires or is otherwise unable to sit as a member of the High Court or is absent, the presiding judge may in his discretion direct that the appeal or application shall proceed before the remaining judges or that a further judge of the High Court be obtained to sit.

In the case in which (a) a decision has been suspended in terms of sub-Section (2) in order to obtain the opinion of a further judge of the High

THE STRUCTURE OF THE COURTS

Court, or b) a further judge of the High Court has been obtained to sit in terms of sub-Section (3), the presiding judge may direct the recalling of any witness or order further argument before the judges who originally constituted the court and the further judge.

4. If a matter being heard by the High Court involves a difficult question of law or if at any stage during the hearing of a matter by one or more judges such a question arises, the presiding judge may direct that the hearing of that matter or the hearing in respect of that question shall proceed before such greater number of judges than two as may be determined by the Chief Justice or the Judge-President, and thereupon the decision of the majority of such judges shall be the decision of the High Court.

The system of assessors came to replace the jury system that was abolished in 1973.[20] The latter had become thoroughly discredited because of its overwhelming racial prejudices: jurors were white and achieved notoriety for acquitting whites in almost all crimes against blacks.[21]

Jurisdiction

Section 23 of the High Court Act makes it clear that the High Court has 'full original criminal jurisdiction over all persons and over all matters in Zimbabwe'. This means that there is no limit to its jurisdiction regarding the nature of the crime, the possible punishment and the place within Zimbabwe where the crime is committed.

Its jurisdiction over persons is limited by Section 30 of the Constitution, which grants the president (while in office) immunity from any 'criminal proceedings whatsoever in any court'.

The High Court's extra-territorial jurisdiction is limited. With statutory crimes, this depends on the provisions of the relevant statute. For example, Section 9 of the Public Order and Security Act (Chapter 11:17) provides as follows:

> Any person who, inside or *outside* Zimbabwe, supplies weaponry to an insurgent, bandit, saboteur or terrorist, knowing that the person to whom such weaponry is supplied is an insurgent, bandit, saboteur or terrorist or realizing that there is a risk or possibility that such person is an insurgent, bandit, saboteur or terrorist, shall be guilty of an offence and liable to imprisonment for life.

It does not have extra-territorial jurisdiction over all common law offences. It has this jurisdiction only in respect of the crime of treason and offences where the harmful effect is felt in Zimbabwe. The leading case on the latter point is *S v Mharapara*, where it was held that the High Court had jurisdiction to try a Zimbabwean diplomat who, while in a foreign country, stole money belonging to the Zimbabwean government.[22]

The High Court also has automatic jurisdiction to review criminal proceedings in the Magistrates Courts wherever any person has been imprisoned for any period in excess of 12 months.[23] It also hears appeals in criminal matters from the Magistrates Court against conviction and/or sentence.[24]

The Supreme Court

The relevant pieces of legislation governing operations of the Supreme Court are the Constitution of Zimbabwe and the Supreme Court Act.[25]

Composition

Under Section 80 of the Constitution, the Supreme Court consists of the Chief Justice, not less than two other judges and any acting judges who may be appointed. The qualifications and manner of appointment of Supreme Court judges are the same as those for the High Court. For exercising its jurisdiction, the Supreme Court is duly constituted if it consists of not less than three judges, one of whom must either be the Chief Justice or a permanent judge of the court.[26] In matters involving the question of the application, enforcement or interpretation or an infringement of the Constitution, the Chief Justice or Minister of Justice may direct that the court be constituted by not less than five judges.[27] In the absence of such a directive, even a matter involving the interpretation of the Constitution may be heard by three judges.

Jurisdiction

The Supreme Court is the final court of appeal in Zimbabwe.[28] It has jurisdiction to hear appeals in criminal cases from any court or tribunal from which, in terms of any Act of Parliament, an appeal lies to it.[29] Under current law, it hears appeals from the High Court and it is no longer permissible to make any direct appeals from the Magistrates Court to the Supreme Court.[30]

The Supreme Court only sits as an appellate court and does not have original jurisdiction. There is *one* exception to this, namely, that it may sit as a first and final court under Section 24 of the Constitution in matters where it is alleged that the Bill of Rights has been or is being infringed. In criminal matters, this could arise where the accused person challenges the constitutionality of his/her arrest and/or prosecution.

Courts-martial

These are established in terms of Section 45 of the Defence Act.[31] The jurisdiction of a court-martial is to try members of the defence forces for any offences in terms of the Act. Some of the offences specified by the Act are common law crimes. Ordinary criminal courts have concurrent jurisdiction over members of the defence forces and this jurisdiction overrides that of the courts-martial. This means that where a member of the defence forces has been tried by a court-martial, he/she may be tried again for that offence by an ordinary court provided the latter court takes into account, for purposes of sentence, any punishment already imposed by the court-martial.[32] The Constitution allows this state of affairs, notwithstanding the protection purportedly granted by Section 18 (b).[33]

Police board of officers

The Police Act allows for a board of officers to try members of the police force who commit offences under the Defence Act.[34] However, the offences may be tried by either an ordinary court or a board of officers, and a member of the police force is entitled to elect to be tried by a Magistrates Court instead of a board of officers.[35]

Prison courts

An officer in the prison service may be tried for some offences by a board appointed by the Commissioner of Prisons.[36] This board cannot impose a sentence of imprisonment, but it may order the dismissal of the officer from employment. Prisoners may also be tried for prison offences by the Commissioner (or his/her delegate), but this is only in respect of minor offences and no sentence of imprisonment may be imposed.[37] In all other respects, prisoners who commit prison offences are tried by either a visiting magistrate (called a 'visiting justice') or the ordinary Magistrates Court.

Children's Courts

Children's courts are established in terms of Section 3 of the Children's Act (Chapter 5:06). These courts used to be called 'juvenile courts' and were renamed in 2001, after the enactment of the Children's Protection and Adoption Amendment Act, 2001 (Act No. 23 of 2001). This Amendment Act also changed the title of the Act from 'Children's Protection and Adoption Act' to 'Children's Act'. The children's court does not try children for criminal offences but may deal with a child who has been convicted by another court. Where no specific children's court has been established by the Minister of Justice, a Magistrates Court serves as a children's court for its area of jurisdiction. In dealing with a convicted child, the children's court has several options. It may order him/her to be placed in a training institute or be placed in the custody of any suitable person, or to attend a specified centre at specified days and for specified hours.[38] The normal procedure is that when a Magistrates Court or High Court convicts a child, it decides whether or not to refer the matter to a children's court. If it decides to refer the matter, then the children's court takes over the matter as explained above.

Parliament sitting as a Court over breach of parliamentary privileges

Parliament enjoys what are called 'privileges' for purposes of enabling it to carry out its constitutional duties effectively. In Zimbabwe, these privileges are regulated by the Privileges, Immunities and Powers of Parliament Act that was passed pursuant to Section 49 of the Constitution of Zimbabwe.[39] Among these privileges are (i) freedom of speech and debate, (ii) exemption from attendance at court whilst in attendance in Parliament and (iii) the right to punish for breach of privilege and contempt of Parliament.[40]

In exercising its right to punish for breach of privilege, Parliament is entitled to sit as a court.[41] Section 16 (4) of the Act provides as follows:

> Parliament sitting as a court shall have all such rights and privileges of a court of record as may be necessary for the purpose of summarily inquiring into and punishing the commission of any act, matter or thing which in this Part is declared to be an offence.

The right extends over both members of Parliament and any member of the public found guilty of contempt of Parliament. The procedure normally followed is that once any member raises a complaint of breach of privilege, the Speaker of Parliament must make a ruling whether or not there is a *prima facie* case. If there is a *prima facie* case, a Privileges Committee is appointed to investigate the complaint. The composition of this committee is in proportion to the representation of political parties in Parliament. Normal practice requires that the person against whom the complaint is made be given a hearing, including legal representation, before the Committee. The Committee will report its findings and recommendations to the whole house, which must in turn resolve whether to accept or reject them. A member found guilty may be suspended or expelled from the House, or even imprisoned.[42] It is this power of imprisonment which makes Parliament a 'criminal court'. There is no right of appeal against conviction or sentence. This is an extraordinary jurisdiction that is difficult to reconcile with modern democratic notions of separation of powers and rule of law. Although the UK Parliament enjoys a similar power, it has been noted that 'no person has been committed to prison for contempt since 1800 (and then only for one night)'.[43] Imprisonment terminates at the end of the session of Parliament in which it was imposed.[44]

Ordinary Civil Courts

Magistrates Courts

Jurisdiction

For purposes of civil cases, the Magistrates Court has the same jurisdiction regardless of the seniority of the magistrate presiding over the matter. In other words, in civil matters, unlike criminal cases, there is no division of magistrates into the four classes of ordinary magistrate, senior magistrate, provincial magistrate and regional magistrate. A Magistrates Court has jurisdiction to apply both customary law and general law in its determination of civil cases.

The general rule is that a Magistrates Court only has jurisdiction in a civil case if (i) the amount claimed does not exceed its prescribed monetary limit of jurisdiction and (ii) either the defendant resides, carries on business, or is employed within the province where the court is situated, or the cause of action arose wholly within the province.[45] The monetary limit is adjusted from time to time.[46] Regardless of the residence of the parties or the place where the cause of action arose, both parties may agree by a memorandum signed by them or their respective legal practitioners that a particular Magistrates Court shall have jurisdiction. Such an agreement is binding on the named Magistrates Court and it shall be obliged to exercise jurisdiction.[47]

There are some civil cases over which the Magistrates Court is prohibited from exercising jurisdiction. These are specified in Section 14 of the Magistrates Court Act and they include (i) disputes in respect of the validity or interpretation of a written will; (ii) the status of a person in respect of mental capacity; and (iii) the dissolution of a marriage other than a marriage solemnized in terms of the Customary Marriages Act (Chapter 5:07).

Composition

In a civil case, the magistrate sits alone. He/she may appoint one or more persons to sit as assessors and assist in an 'advisory capacity'. Any such appointment requires the approval of the Minister of Justice.[48] The person appointed must be willing to serve and have skill and experience in any matter to be considered by the court. Unlike in a criminal case, an assessor appointed in a civil case merely sits to advise and has no voice in the findings of the court on both matters of fact and of law. In practice, it is rare in Zimbabwe for assessors to be appointed in civil cases.

The High Court

Composition

In civil cases, the judge sits alone. He/she may also appoint one or more persons to sit as an assessor or assessors and assist in an 'advisory capacity'.[49] As in the Magistrates Court, an assessor appointed in a civil case must be willing to serve and have skill and experience in any matter to be considered. Section 5 (2) of the High Court Act makes it clear that such an assessor 'shall act in an advisory capacity only and shall not be entitled to vote in the decision of the court'.

Jurisdiction

Section 13 of the High Court Act states that the High Court 'shall have full original civil jurisdiction over all persons and over all matters within Zimbabwe'. This means that its original jurisdiction is unlimited; there are no monetary limits to claims that may be brought; and it can hear any civil dispute, whatever the nature of the claim. It enjoys what is called 'inherent jurisdiction', which means that the High Court is deemed to have jurisdiction unless so prohibited by some law. This kind of jurisdiction is superior to that of any other court because all other courts can only exercise the jurisdiction specifically granted by the enabling statute.

The fact that the High Court's original jurisdiction is unlimited means that all matters which may be heard by the Magistrates Court can also, at first instance, be heard by the High Court. A litigant is entitled to sue in the High Court, even in matters within the monetary limit of the Magistrates Court. The High Court can only refuse to entertain a case if there is a law that prohibits it from exercising jurisdiction. The choice of court may be dictated by costs; it is more expensive to sue in the High Court than in the Magistrates Court. Thus, for small claims, it may make little economic sense to use the High Court.

The High Court also has 'appellate jurisdiction' in civil cases. An appeal only goes to the High Court if there is a specific provision in a statute granting a right of appeal to the High Court. Appeals from the Magistrates Court go to the High Court.[50]

Apart from being an appellate court, the High Court has inherent review powers over the proceedings of all inferior courts and tribunals.[51] A review is not concerned with the merits of the decision but with the decision-making process. In exercising its review powers, the High Court may set aside proceedings of an inferior court or tribunal.

The Supreme Court
Composition

The Supreme Court is considered duly constituted if it consists of not less than three judges, one of whom shall be either the Chief Justice or a permanent judge of the court.[52] It may be composed of two judges when hearing an appeal from any court other than the High Court, provided this happens on the directions of the Chief Justice.[53] If an appeal involves a difficult or important question of law, the presiding judge may direct that the appeal be heard by a greater number of judges. In such cases, the Chief Justice shall determine the size of the reconstituted court.[54] In a matter involving the application or interpretation of the Constitution, the Chief Justice or the Minister may direct that the court be composed of not less than five judges.[55]

The minimum number of judges who must be appointed to the Supreme Court is three.[56] There is no maximum number. The number of judges at any one time is determined by the president.[57] The choice of which judges sit in a particular matter is determined by the Chief Justice and it appears that his/her choice cannot be challenged in court.[58]

Jurisdiction

The Supreme Court has appellate jurisdiction only in civil matters, except where the issue is brought under Section 24 of the Constitution. An appeal only lies with the Supreme Court where the provisions of the relevant statute say so. In respect of appeals from the High Court, there is a right of appeal to the Supreme Court from any judgment, even if it arises from the High Court's exercise of its original or appellate jurisdiction.[59] The only circumstance where an appeal from the High Court is barred is where the judgment in question was obtained with the consent of the parties.[60]

Specialist Courts

Specialist courts only deal with areas that have been deemed by Parliament to require a 'special court'. In other words, a specialist court deals with a specific issue. A common example of a specialist court is the Labour Court, which deals with labour disputes only. Other important examples of specialist courts are the Income Tax Court and the Administrative Court. The law-maker has also created two courts that administer 'customary law' only and these are by definition specialist courts.

Advantages of specialist courts in Zimbabwe

Ordinary courts deal with all sorts of cases and therefore tend to be overloaded with cases. A person wishing to approach the ordinary court is usually faced with a delay before his/her case can be heard. By contrast, no such delay should be faced in a properly functioning system of specialist courts. Since a specialist court deals only with specified issues, it should be less loaded than the ordinary court, and hence it should be quicker to have a case heard in the specialist court than in the ordinary court. Specialist courts should therefore deliver justice more quickly.

Additionally, ordinary courts invariably adopt procedures that are complicated, confusing and generally only understood by lawyers. This works adversely against a person who is not represented by a lawyer. By contrast, most specialist courts adopt informal procedures that are flexible and therefore capable of being understood by the layperson. This flexibility and simplicity is conducive to the delivery of justice.

In view of the complexity of procedures before ordinary courts, lawyers are almost invariably a necessity. This, together with the delays experienced, make proceedings before ordinary courts expensive. Accordingly, the general absence of delays and, sometimes, the lack of necessity for legal representation make proceedings before specialist courts cheaper than in ordinary courts.

Moreover, an ordinary court may fail to deliver justice by failing to appreciate the specialist aspects of an issue. It may have to rely on conflicting expert evidence. This is avoided in specialist courts, which, by definition, should be sensitive to any specific issues and therefore capable of administering justice from an informed perspective. For instance, a tax court should be better able to administer justice between parties to a taxation dispute than the ordinary court.

Disadvantages of specialist courts

While the above advantages have led to the establishment of specialist courts, they do have some disadvantages. For example:

The informal nature of proceedings may actually lead to injustice where principles of natural justice are compromised.

The jurisdiction of specialist courts is limited and there is always the fear that proceedings may be set aside by the High Court for lack of jurisdiction.

Some specialist courts involve some complex issues such that the ordinary person cannot utilize their services without the aid of specialists. An example would be the Income Tax Court and Patents Tribunal.

Examples of specialist courts

The Labour Court

The law that governs employment of workers in Zimbabwe is largely contained in the Labour Act (Chapter 28:01). It is this Act that enables the creation of a special court known as the Labour Court, whose main function is to administer justice that is sensitive to the plight of workers. This court *only* deals with labour disputes. The Labour Court was established in March 2003 and replaced the Labour Relations Tribunal. It was introduced by the Labour Relations Amendment Act, 2002 (Act No. 17 of 2002).

The jurisdiction of the Labour Court is specified in Section 89 of the Labour Act. In general, it is an appeal court for a variety of labour disputes. In a few cases, it is a court of 'first instance'. An example of the latter is where a dispute may arise in relation to the extent or description of any undertaking or industry represented by a trade union. Such a dispute may be referred directly to the Labour Court for determination.[61] As an appeal court, the Labour Court is involved in two main situations.

The first situation relates to labour disputes that are referred to conciliation and/or arbitration. Under the Labour Act, most labour disputes that remain unresolved after conciliation by a labour officer are required to be referred to arbitration. After arbitration, the Labour Court comes in to hear any appeal 'on a question of law' on any decisions of the arbitrator.[62]

The second situation is where the Labour Court hears appeals from decisions made in terms of an employment code registered under Section 101 of the Act. The employer(s) and employee(s) in an industry undertaking or work place may register an employment code providing for the disciplinary rules to be observed in the industry, undertaking or workplace concerned, the procedures to be followed in the event of a breach of the code and the penalties for any breach of the code. Once an employment code has been registered, all misconduct disputes have to be dealt with in terms of the code. Appeals from the final decision made in terms of the code go to the Labour Court.

The Labour Court has exclusive jurisdiction over the matters specified in Section 89 of the Act. Section 89 (6) provides as follows:

> No court, other than the Labour Court, shall have jurisdiction in the first instance to hear and determine any application, appeal or matter referred to in sub-Section (1).

An appeal to the Labour Court should be made within 14 days of any decision. The appeal requires the appellant to fill in the appropriate form. These simple forms need not be completed by a legal practitioner. They may also be completed on behalf of a worker by a trade union official.

The Labour Relations Tribunal, which preceded the Labour Court, consisted of a chairman, who was a person qualified to be a High Court judge, a deputy chairman (who had to be a registered legal practitioner) and up to four other members who were either legal practitioners or persons experienced in labour relations. The Tribunal could be constituted by one member sitting alone or by two or more members. It was required by law to be informal in its proceedings and thus was not bound by the rigid rules of evidence that apply in ordinary courts. A worker, besides the entitlement to represent herself/himself, could also be represented by a member of the workers' committee or trade union.

The Labour Court is different in a number of respects. Its composition is specified in Section 84 of the Labour Act. It consists of a Senior president, several presidents of the court and assessors. The Senior president and presidents of the court are appointed by the president of Zimbabwe after consultation with the Judicial Service Commission. A person is qualified for appointment as a president of the Labour Court if he/she is a former judge of the Supreme Court or the High Court, or is qualified to be a judge of the High Court, or has been a magistrate in Zimbabwe for not less than seven years. Assessors are appointed by the Senior president of the Court in consultation with the Minister of Justice. An assessor must be a person who has 'knowledge or experience in labour relations'. Assessors have no voice in the decision of any question of law or any question as to whether a matter for decision is a question of fact or law or any question as to the admissibility of evidence.[63]

An appeal from any decision of the Labour Court lies to the Supreme Court, but only on a question of law.

The Administrative Court

The Administrative Court is a specialist court that deals with a number of issues allocated to it by various pieces of legislation. It is set up in terms of the Administrative Court Act (Chapter 7:01) and consists of a president of the Court, who, once again, is either a former judge of the High Court or Supreme Court, a person qualified for appointment as such, or a person who has been a magistrate for at least seven years, and assessors.

Various pieces of legislation allocate functions to the Administrative Court. These include (i) the Land Acquisition Act (Chapter 20:10), which gives the court in Section 7 the power to authorize or confirm acquisition of land to which there has been an objection by the owner; and (ii) the Regional, Town and Country Planning Act (Chapter 29:12), which gives the court various functions to resolve disputes between local planning authorities and any persons aggrieved by the former's proposed use of land or refusal to grant permits for development of land for certain purposes (see, for instance, Sections 11, 38 and 41). The most common function of the Administrative Court is being the Water Court for purposes of the Water Act (Chapter 20:22). This requires some more detailed explanation.

The Administrative Court as the Water Court

There used to be a separate Water Court that regulated the use of public water among competing interests in Zimbabwe. From December 1979, all the functions of the old Water Court were taken over by the Administrative Court. However, it is still correct to refer to the Administrative Court as the 'Water Court' whenever it is performing these functions. In terms of the Water Act, the Administrative Court is the only court to which a dispute concerning the use of public water may be referred.

To understand the importance of the Administrative Court as a Water Court, it is necessary to briefly outline the law governing rights to the use of water in Zimbabwe. The law is largely contained in the Water Act (Chapter 20:22). Water in Zimbabwe is divided into three groups: private water, public water and underground water. Private water refers to water that rises naturally on any land and remains on the surface of the land without joining a public stream. Public water refers to water found on or below the bed of a public stream. Underground water is all water that is beneath the surface of the ground.

Private water is owned by the owner of the land on which it is found and that owner has the sole right to its exclusive use. He/she does not need to apply to court to obtain the permission of any public authority to use the water for any particular purpose. On the other hand, public water and underground water are legally owned by the president of Zimbabwe. No person has a legal right to use that water outside the provisions of the Water Act.

The Act grants any person in Zimbabwe the right to use public water for cooking, drinking or washing, without the need for court authorization. Further, any person who owns land along which a public stream or river passes (such a person is technically called a 'riparian owner' and the land 'riparian land') has a right to use the public water in the stream or river for limited purposes in addition to the purposes of cooking, drinking or washing. Such limited purposes include gardening, support of animal life and brick-making.

Outside these two situations, the right to use public water for agricultural, electrical, and a host of other purposes requires the authorization of the Administrative Court. Any person can apply to this court for the right to use public water for stated purposes. Once the right is given, the holder of the right has preferential use of this public water.

The holder of the right becomes, for all intents and purposes, the 'owner' of the water and may use it to the exclusion of others who have not been granted a right. It is precisely because most large-scale commercial farmers have water rights over most public water in Zimbabwe that small-scale commercial farmers (mainly Africans) have been unable to utilize water in some public streams for the benefit of their own agricultural activities. It is this aspect of granting right over a key natural resource as water that makes the Administrative Court a court of strategic importance.

An application for a water right may be lodged at any time with the Registrar of the Administrative Court, who will thereafter place it before the court. In considering the application, the latter is required to take into account the extent and nature of all land irrigable by the water concerned and may, in view of that consideration, impose conditions on any right it grants. A typical example would be a limit on the amount of water that can be used in order to ensure a supply for other users.

More significantly, the court is required by the Act to be satisfied that all persons who may be adversely affected by the grant of a water right have been given due notice of the application and, if they so wish, have been allowed to make representations and arguments before the court. It is clear that the persons staying in the community through which a public stream passes would have an interest in any rights that may be granted to any person over the public water.

A person appearing before the Administrative Court may be represented by a legal practitioner, but may also appear in person or may also be represented by any other, as long as that person has been appointed in writing by the party concerned. Thus, a party may be represented by a friend or any other person who is not legally qualified, something that is not permissible in an ordinary court.

Appeals from the Administrative Court go to the Supreme Court.

Special court for income tax appeals

Taxation issues raise complicated problems. A taxpayer may be unhappy with an assessment made upon him/her. For example, he/she may feel that they have been asked to pay more tax than is legally due or be aggrieved by a decision of the Commissioner of Taxes. The Income Tax Act (Chapter 23:06) allows for a special court to hear appeals from taxpayers who feel that they have not been viewed fairly.

The special court for Income Tax Appeals is presided over by a president of the Court, again either a former judge of the High Court or Supreme Court, or a person qualified to be appointed a judge of the High Court or Supreme Court. The president of the Court sits with assessors whose role is purely advisory. The decision of the Court lies exclusively with the presiding judge.

The most common grounds for appeals to this court by taxpayers are where the tax assessment is being queried on the basis of being excessive or where the taxpayer is arguing that no liability to tax arises at all. It is important to note, however, that a taxpayer is also entitled to appeal to the High Court instead of the Special Court for income tax appeals, if he/she so wishes. The High Court enjoys the same jurisdiction as the Special

Court for Income Tax Appeals. The advantage of choosing to appeal to the Special Court for income tax appeals is that a tax payer is entitled, before that court, to be represented by a person who is not a legal practitioner as long as the person has been appointed in writing. This enables a taxpayer to be represented by a tax expert. In the High Court, however, there can only be legal representation or representation in person.

A taxpayer making an appeal to the Special Court should do so by lodging with it, in writing, a notice of appeal within 21 days of receiving a notice from the Commissioner confirming an assessment or decision. This period may be extended by the Special Court on good cause shown. Within 60 days of receiving the taxpayer's grounds of appeal, the Commissioner is required to state his/her case and relay it to this Special Court.

The parties involved may call witnesses and lead such evidence as they may deem relevant before the Special Court makes its decision. Decisions of the Special Court on questions of law can be appealed, as of right, to the Supreme Court of Zimbabwe. Special leave (permission) is required if the appeal is based on fact alone or on a mixture of law and facts.

Local courts on customary law

Customary law disputes may be referred to special courts that have been established to preserve the application of customary law in civil disputes. There are two types of local courts, namely (i) a primary court that is presided over by a headman or other person appointed by the Minister of Justice and (ii) a community court, which is presided over by a Chief or other person appointed by the Minister of Justice. Both courts are established in terms of the Customary Law and Local Courts Act (Chapter 7:05).

The main reason for the existence of these customary law courts is to provide ordinary people in rural areas with a justice system that is consistent with African custom and values. A large number of ordinary Zimbabweans regulate their lives in accordance with customary law. For that reason, the legal system has preserved the authority of traditional leaders to adjudicate in civil disputes governed by customary law. The following points must be noted:

- The court can only apply customary law and nothing else.
- The local court is not permitted to adjudicate particular disputes, even though such disputes are governed by customary law. For example, it is not permitted to adjudicate matters involving the dissolution of a customary law marriage solemnized in terms of the Customary Marriage Act (Chapter 5:07); the determination of custody or guardianship of

THE STRUCTURE OF THE COURTS

minors; the determination of maintenance claims; and determination of any rights in respect of land.

- A local court has jurisdiction to hear a case only if either the defendant is resident in the local area of the court or the case took place within the local area (that is, the cause of action arose in the local area) or the defendant has agreed that the court should have jurisdiction.
- A party wishing to take a case to a local court simply has to approach the Clerk of Court concerned and be assisted with sending a summons. The summons may be served on the other party by either the Messenger of Court or the Police.
- The procedure adopted in local courts is very informal and is determined by customary law. Lawyers are not permitted in local courts.
- A judgment given by a local court is enforceable by first registering it with a Magistrates Court and thereafter enforcing it like any other Magistrates Court judgment. This means that it can be enforced by execution of property, contempt of court proceedings, garnishee order or civil imprisonment.
- An appeal from the primary court presided over by a headman goes to the community court presided over by a Chief. A further appeal may be made to a Magistrates Court and thereafter to the High Court and Supreme Court of Zimbabwe. A case involving the payment of damages can either start in the primary court or in the community court depending on the amount claimed.
- The value of a claim before a local court should not exceed specified amounts.
- Where the amount claimed is more than the specified amount, local courts have no jurisdiction and the case has to be initiated in a Magistrates Court.

Small Claims Court

A person who has a small claim to make against another is saved the inconvenience and delay of approaching the ordinary courts by being able to approach the Small Claims Courts. These courts are established in terms of the Small Claims Court Act (Chapter 7:12). The power to establish a Small Claims Court in any province is given to the Minister of Justice, Legal and Parliamentary Affairs. The most important points about a Small Claims Court are as follows:

- A claim that may be referred to a Small Claims Court should not exceed the specified amount.[64]

THE STRUCTURE OF THE COURTS

- A Small Claims Court has no jurisdiction whatsoever to hear certain matters, namely, claims involving customary law; claims for divorce or custody of a minor; maintenance claims (although it may hear a claim for arrears maintenance); the interpretation of wills; and claims for defamation, adultery or seduction.
- Only individuals can bring proceedings before Small Claims Courts. Companies or other bodies can only be sued but cannot sue in a Small Claims Court.
- Lawyers are not allowed to represent litigants in a Small Claims Court.
- For a Small Claims Court to have jurisdiction, the defendant has to be either a resident or be running a business in the province. Outside the two situations, the court can only have jurisdiction if the defendant does not object to jurisdiction.
- To commence proceedings, the person wishing to institute proceedings (the plaintiff) should first send a letter of demand to the defendant giving the latter 14 days to settle the claim. It is only if his/her demand is not honoured that the plaintiff may request the Clerk of the Small Claims Court to issue summons against the defendant. The summons shall specify the claim and the date of the hearing and may be served on the defendant personally by the plaintiff, or if the plaintiff pays a fee, by the Messenger of Court.
- Any person bringing or defending proceedings before a Small Claims Court is entitled to assistance in the preparation of his/her documents by a legal assistant attached to the Small Claims Court.
- A judgment given by the Small Claims Court is final and cannot be appealed against, except to take the proceedings on review to the High Court.
- Where the defendant has failed to satisfy the judgment given by the Small Claims Court, the plaintiff (now judgment creditor) may apply to the Clerk of Court for the issue of a writ of execution against property. This is the only way of enforcing the judgment of a Small Claims Court.

Notes

1. See Section 6 of the Magistrates Court Act.
2. See Section 52 of the Constitution of Zimbabwe.
3. Ibid., Section 52 (1) (b).
4. Ibid.
5. Ibid., Section 52 (3) (e).

THE STRUCTURE OF THE COURTS

6. Ibid., Section 52 (3) (e).
7. Ibid., See Section 56 (6).
8. Ibid., Section 56 for the exceptions.
9. Ibid., Section 49 (1).
10. Ibid., Section 49 (2).
11. Ibid., Section 51 (1).
12. Chapter 7:06.
13. See Section 3 (b) of the Constitution of Zimbabwe.
14. Ibid., Section 3 (d).
15. See Section 6 (1) (d).
16. See Section 6 (2).
17. See Section 6 (3).
18. See Section 10 (2). A high profile example of such a situation was in *S v Tekere*, 1980 ZLR 489.
19. See Section 10 (4) of the Constitution of Zimbabwe.
20. See Criminal Procedure and Evidence Amendment Act, 1973 (Act No. 32 of 1973), Section 2.
21. For a discussion of the jury system, see (1992) 109 *SALJ* 679; (1993) 110 *SALJ* 333.
22. 1985 (2) *ZLR* 211 (S).
23. Section 57 (1) of the Magistrates Court Act.
24. Ibid., Section 60 (1).
25. Chapter 7:13.
26. See Section 3 of the Supreme Court Act.
27. Ibid. See proviso (iii) to Section 3.
28. See Section 80 (1) of the Constitution of Zimbabwe.
29. See Section 9 (1) of the Supreme Court Act.
30. Amendments to this effect were made by the Magistrates Court Amendment Act, 1997 (Act No. 9 of 1997).
31. See Chapter 11:02.
32. See Sections 56 (2) and 57 (1).
33. See the exception in 18 (13) (d).
34. See Chapter 11:10.
35. See Section 32.
36. See the Prisons (Staff) (Discipline) Regulations, 1984 (ST 289/1984).
37. See the schedule to the Prison Act (Chapter 7:11).
38. See Section 20 of the Children's Act.
39. See Chapter 2:08.
40. Privileges, Immunities and Powers of Parliament Act, Section 3.
41. Ibid., Section 16.
42. Ibid., Section 32.
43. See Stanley de Smith and Rodney Brazier (1999), *Constitutional and Administrative Law*. Eighth edition. UK: Penguin Books, p. 328.

THE STRUCTURE OF THE COURTS

44. See Section 32 (1) of the Privileges, Immunities and Powers of Parliament Act.
45. See Section 11 (1) (a) of the Magistrates Court Act.
46. See the Magistrates Court (Civil Jurisdiction) (Monetary Limits) Rules, 2004 (SI 160 of 2004).
47. See Section 11 (1) (c) of the Magistrates Court Act.
48. Ibid., Section 16.
49. See Section 5 of the High Court Act.
50. See Section 40 of the Magistrates Court Act.
51. See Section 26 of the High Court Act.
52. See Section 3 of the Supreme Court Act.
53. Ibid. See proviso (i) to Section 3.
54. Ibid. See proviso (ii) to Section 3.
55. Ibid. See proviso (iii) to Section 3.
56. See Section 80 of the Constitution of Zimbabwe.
57. Ibid.
58. See *Minister of Lands & Ors v Commercial Farmers Union* 2001 (2) ZLR 457 (S), 462D.
59. See Section 43 of the High Court Act.
60. Ibid.
61. See Section 46 of the Labour Act.
62. Ibid., Section 98 (10).
63. Ibid., Section 90.
64. See Small Claims Courts (Jurisdiction) Notice, 2004 (SI 159/2004).

6

The Legal Profession in Zimbabwe

Introduction: The legal profession

A leading English textbook opens its chapter on the legal profession in the following way:

> The title 'Lawyer' is reserved for those who have received the special status of membership of the 'legal profession'. It is not a straightforward job description: many non-lawyers perform legal tasks, some of them full-time. For example, accountants may specialize in revenue law, trade union officials may appear regularly before industrial tribunals on behalf of their members and solicitors may delegate work to legal executives and paralegals. Conversely, many of the tasks performed by lawyers are not strictly 'legal'.[1]

The legal profession is a profession in the sense that it has the following characteristics that are generally regarded as defining a profession:

- It has a governing body with powers of control and discipline.
- There is some register or record of membership.
- There is restriction of admission to those with the required standard of special skills, education and training.
- There is voluntary submission by members to standards of ethical conduct beyond those required of the ordinary citizen by law.
- The duty to clients is paramount.[2]

A divided or fused profession?

Under the English system, the legal profession is divided into two branches: a lawyer is either a solicitor or a barrister. Each branch has its own training requirements, customs of practice and traditions. A solicitor is a general practitioner who deals with clients directly while a barrister cannot, in general, deal directly with clients but must be engaged by a solicitor. Although a barrister may be involved in legal drafting and writing legal opinions/advice for a solicitor, he/she is primarily a court advocate. The general approach is that solicitors deal directly with clients in a wide range of services and engage barristers either to appear and argue cases in superior courts or to provide specialist advice.

Prior to the Courts and Legal Service Act 1990, solicitors had no right of audience in all superior courts and barristers thus enjoyed a virtual monopoly of advocacy in these courts. The current legal position is that both barristers and solicitors have a right of audience before every court. However, this is subject to meeting the prescribed training requirements: completing pupilage in the case of barristers and obtaining a higher courts advocacy qualification in the case of solicitors. In practice, many solicitors choose not to obtain the higher courts advocacy qualification. Accordingly, it is mainly barristers who have the right of audience in the superior courts. Solicitors work either as sole solicitors or in partnership. Barristers are not permitted to form partnerships. Instead, they work in groups of offices known as 'chambers'.

Other legal systems that have a divided legal profession use different terminology. For example, in the US, the two branches of the legal profession are *attorneys* and *advocates.* Attorneys are the equivalent of English solicitors while advocates are the equivalent of barristers. It is important to emphasize that while the terms 'attorney' and 'advocate' are used, their difference from solicitors and barristers is in name only. South Africa has a divided profession and uses the terminology of attorneys and advocates.

In Zimbabwe, the legal profession is no longer divided into two branches. It may therefore be described as a 'fused' profession. Prior to 1981, the profession was divided into two branches: attorneys and advocates. Attorneys dealt directly with the members of the public as clients while advocates were not permitted to do so. An advocate could only be instructed by an attorney. Attorneys had no right of audience in the superior courts (the High Court and the Supreme Court): this was the exclusive preserve of advocates.

The main argument in defence of a divided profession is premised on the quality of legal services. A divided profession leads to the growth of specialization by advocates. These specialist advocates are at the disposal of a 'queue' of attorneys/solicitors from different firms and this enhances the quality of legal services to clients. Further, there is what has been termed the 'principle of judicial unpreparedness' – the judge has no research staff and relies on the parties to present their cases thoroughly. In such circumstances, it is important to promote the system of a separate group of specialist advocates. However, given the nature of court procedures in Zimbabwe, which tend to rely more on oral rather than written presentations of argument, hearings tend to be lengthy. This creates enormous inconveniences for lawyers, thus creating the need for an organized group of advocates with the appropriate legal capacity.

In 1981 Zimbabwe's legal profession was fused via the Legal Practitioners Act, 1981 (Act No. 15 of 1981), now Chapter 27:07. A prominent argument in favour of this fusion was political. At that time, close to 99 per cent of advocates were white. As the right of audience in the superior courts was limited to advocates, this meant that advocacy in the superior courts was limited to white lawyers. This was, in the new political dispensation, neither acceptable nor desirable. The new government had unveiled a policy of 'Black Advancement' and fusing the legal profession was viewed as a key component of this policy. Besides this political argument, there were other standard arguments in favour of fusion. A divided profession is expensive in that a client may have to pay for two lawyers: the attorney/solicitor and an advocate/barrister if the case needs to be heard in a superior court. Further, it is also said that a divided profession causes inefficiency, largely due to failures of communication between the attorney and the advocate; it may also arise from inevitable delays by advocates/barristers.

The nature of the fused profession in Zimbabwe

All lawyers entitled to practice the profession of law fall into the category of 'legal practitioner'. Every registered legal practitioner has a right of audience in any court in which persons are entitled by law to legal representation. However, there are two specialist practices of the legal profession that are not available to every registered legal practitioner. These are notarial practice and conveyancing. To be able to engage in either of these two, a registered legal practitioner must also be registered as a notary public or conveyancer or both. One may be a legal practitioner without being a conveyancer or a notary public.

There are, therefore, four possibilities for a legal practitioner:
1. A legal practitioner only (with neither the right to practice as a notary public nor that of being a conveyancer).
2. A legal practitioner, notary public and conveyancer.
3. A legal practitioner and notary public.
4. A legal practitioner and conveyancer.

Notarial practice mainly involves the execution, attestation and authentication of documents that are required by law to be executed, attested or authenticated by a notary public. Conveyancing involves preparation and execution of documents relating to the transfer of rights in land and either registrable in the Deeds Registry or requiring attestation or execution by a registrar of deeds.

In practice, there exists a *de facto* divided profession in Zimbabwe, as there are lawyers who practice as advocates and voluntarily regulate themselves in the same way as advocates/ barristers in a divided system.

Admission as a legal practitioner

Section 5 of the Legal Practitioners Act sets out six requirements for admission as a legal practitioner. An applicant for registration must:
- Comply with the *formalities* prescribed by law.
- Possess educational qualifications prescribed in rules made by the Council for Legal Education.
- Be normally resident in Zimbabwe or a reciprocating country, or alternatively be granted a residential exemption certificate.
- Be of or above the age of 21.
- Be not an unrehabilitated insolvent.
- Be a fit and proper person.

The formalities referred to are prescribed in the regulations made from time to time. The current regulations are the Legal Practitioners (General) Regulations, 1999 (SI 137 of 1999). The prescribed formalities are that an applicant must give not less than 30 days notice to the Secretary of the Law Society before making an application for registration. The notice must be accompanied by relevant documents, such as the applicant's birth certificate and university degree certificates or transcripts. The prescribed fee must also be enclosed. The Council for Legal Education has prescribed educational qualifications for registration. These are set out in the Legal Practitioners (Council for Legal Education) Rules, 1992 (SI 447 of 1992). There are two sets of educational qualifications:

1. Possession of a designated legal qualification.
2. Passing or being exempted from professional examinations.

A 'designated legal qualification' is a degree or diploma or certificate in law designated by the Council for Legal Education itself. Under the current notice, the law degrees of the following universities are designated: University of Zimbabwe; Midlands State University; the Universities of Zambia, Botswana, Lesotho and Swaziland; any university in South Africa; and any university or other institution of higher education in the United Kingdom. The current notice is the Legal Practitioners (Designated Legal Qualifications) Notice, 2007. A person with a designated legal qualification must either pass or be exempted from professional examinations administered by the Council for Legal Education. For purposes of registration as a Legal Practitioner, holders of an LLB from the University of Zimbabwe are exempt from all professional examinations. In other words, an LLB graduate from the University of Zimbabwe automatically qualifies for registration as a legal practitioner.[3] Holders of all other law degrees do not enjoy a blanket exemption from professional examinations: any such holder seeking an exemption must apply to the Council for Legal Education, which may grant an exemption in one or more papers if satisfied that there is justification for the exemption.[4]

The professional examinations cover up to seven papers in such subjects as the common law of Zimbabwe, civil practice and procedure, law of evidence, interpretation of statutes and book-keeping.[5] A person who is not exempted from professional examinations must pass these examinations before he/she can be registered as a legal practitioner. There are additional educational qualifications for those intending to be notaries public and conveyancers. For holders of University of Zimbabwe law degrees, an applicant must have passed, as part of the degree, course in notarial practice and or conveyancing. For all other applicants, they must either pass or be exempted from professional examinations in notarial practice and/or conveyancing.

Finally, notwithstanding satisfying all other requirements, an applicant must still be a 'fit and proper person'. This expression was explained by the Supreme Court in *In re Chikweche* as follows:

> Construed in context, in my view, the words 'fit and proper person' allude,

in my view, to the personal qualities of an applicant – that he is a person of honesty and reliability.

In *In re Chikweche*, the applicant applied to the High Court for registration as a legal practitioner. He kept his hair in 'dreadlocks'. The judge hearing the application considered that his dreadlocks made him not a 'fit and proper person' and declined to register him. The applicant approached the Supreme Court, challenging this refusal as an infringement of his freedom of conscience and religion as protected by Section 19 of the Constitution. The court held that Rastafarianism was indeed a belief protected by Section 19 of the Constitution and therefore the refusal by the High Court to register the applicant was an infringement of his rights under Section 19. It ordered the registration of the applicant. It was in the context of these facts that the Supreme Court emphasized that the words 'fit and proper person' do not 'embrace' the physical characteristics of an applicant.[6]

Practical legal training after registration

In general, there is no legal requirement that lawyers undergo further training after being admitted into practice. However, there is requirement for additional training whenever a legal practitioner wishes to practice as a principal, either on his/her own account or in partnership with another or others. To be entitled to practice as a principal, a legal practitioner must have been employed as a legal assistant for not less than 36 months. Further, he/she must have:

- Attended a full course of seminars for continuous legal education organized by the Council for Legal Education
- Passed written examinations set by either the Council for Legal Education or the Law Society (with the approval of the Council for Legal Education) in trust accounting, practice management and administration and ethics.

Though contained in SI 137/1999, these further requirements have yet to be put into effect (although these requirements are already law, the law itself is temporarily not in force).

Discipline for professional misconduct

The Law Society of Zimbabwe has the power to deal with professional misconduct by lawyers. The Legal Practitioners Act uses the expression 'unprofessional, dishonourable or unworthy conduct' to refer to professional misconduct. This is a wide term and covers almost every conceivable form of misconduct. Cases of professional misconduct are referred to the Disciplinary Tribunal set up in terms of Section 24 of the Act. A legal practitioner who is found guilty of professional misconduct by the Disciplinary Tribunal may suffer one or more of the following measures:

- Deletion of his/her name from the register of legal practitioners.
- Suspension from legal practice for a specified period.
- Imposition of conditions under which he/she may continue to practice.
- Being censured.
- Being cautioned.[7]

A legal practitioner whose name has been deleted from the register may apply to the High Court to have his/her name restored to the register, provided he/she proves that he/she is fit and proper again. Such an application requires the support of the Law Society.[8]

The Law Society of Zimbabwe

The Law Society is the legal profession's governing body that is set up in terms of Section 51 of the Legal Practitioners Act. Every registered legal practitioner is entitled to be a member. The society is managed and controlled by a council that is composed of not less than eleven councillors, of whom at least nine are elected by members. The remaining minority is appointed by the Minister of Justice. As the majority of the membership is elected, there is adequate scope for the council to be independent. The councillors, once elected, in turn elect, from among themselves, a president and a vice-president. The function and powers of the Law Society are specified in Section 53 of the Act and include:

- Keeping registers of the names and addresses of registered legal practitioners.
- Representing the views of the legal profession and maintaining its integrity and status.
- Defining and enforcing correct and uniform practice and discipline among legal practitioners.
- Promoting social intercourse between legal practitioners.
- Considering and dealing with all matters affecting the professional interests of the legal practitioners.
- Encouraging and promoting the study of law and jurisprudence and

providing means of securing efficiency and responsibility on the part of those seeking registration.

The Council for Legal Education

This council is set up in terms of Section 34 of the Legal Practitioners Act. It is composed of a chairperson and seven other members. The chairperson is nominated by the Chief Justice and appointed by the Minister of Justice. He/she must be a person who is or has been a judge of the Supreme Court or High Court. Of the seven, five members are appointed as follows: the Attorney General (one member), the Faculty of Law of the University of Zimbabwe (two members), and the Law Society (two members). The remaining two members are appointed from persons employed in the Ministry of Justice.

The functions of the Council for Legal Education are as follows:

1. To ensure the maintenance of appropriate standards in legal education and training in Zimbabwe.
2. To determine the qualifications for registration.
3. To determine syllabi for and to set professional examinations to qualify persons for registration.
4. To consider and grant or refuse applications from professional seeking exemption from professional examinations.

In order to exercise these functions, the Council is given powers to:

a) Consider the content and standard of legal qualifications granted inside and outside Zimbabwe.
b) Provide courses of study and training for persons who wish to be registered.
c) Advise the Minister of Justice and any educational institutions concerned on all matters relating to legal education and training.
d) Review legislation relating to legal qualifications, education and training and to advise the Minister of Justice on amendments.

Judges

The process of appointment of judges is a key factor in guaranteeing the independence of the judiciary. Where the appointment process is entirely in the hands of politicians, the likelihood is high that judges will be appointed on the basis of political allegiance thus creating a judiciary which is unlikely to be independent of the executive. On the other hand, judges cannot appoint themselves. To be legitimate, judicial authority must be derived from the people and this necessarily requires, at the very least, that judges be appointed by an elected organ of the state. Politicians are therefore unavoidable. The question in each case becomes one of the extent to which the appointment process has sufficient checks and balances against purely political appointments.[9]

Who appoints judges?

In terms of Section 84 of the Constitution of Zimbabwe, judges are appointed by the president. The checks against purely political appointments by the president are weak. These are (i) that the president must consult the Judicial Service Commission before making the appointment; and (ii) where the proposed appointment is inconsistent with the recommendations of the Judicial Service Commission, the president is required to inform Parliament 'as soon as is practicable'.[10]

The Judicial Service Commission is itself composed of five or six persons, the overwhelming majority of whom are appointed by the president. Three are ex-officio: the Chief Justice or, in his/her absence, a judge of the Supreme Court; the Attorney General; and the Public Service Commission chairperson. The other two/three members are appointed by the president. Although the Constitution insists that one of the three be either a judge or a legal practitioner, it allows the president to ignore this requirement and appoint all three from an undefined group of persons meeting the following vague descriptions:

> [That they] possesses such legal qualifications and [have] had such legal experience as the President considers suitable and adequate for [their] appointment to the Judicial Service Commission.

And:

> Other members shall be chosen for their ability and experience in administration or their professional qualifications or their suitability otherwise for appointment.[11]

With this composition, a powerful president is unlikely to meet an adverse position from the Judicial Service Commission if he/she were to insist on his/her choice.

In the unlikely event of a disagreement, the president is obliged to inform Parliament as soon as is practicable, even though the latter cannot affect the appointment. Under Zimbabwe's presidential system, Parliament has no power over the president except through the medium of an impeachment.[12]

The deference to the executive in the appointment of judges is a post-independence creation, mainly brought about by the Constitution of Zimbabwe Amendment No. 7. This amendment introduced the executive presidency that demolished most of the checks and balances of the Lancaster House framework. In the Lancaster House Constitution, checks against purely political appointments were contained in three main provisions. First, the most powerful politician, the Prime Minister, was not empowered to appoint judges. Appointments were the responsibility of a non-executive head of state. However, the latter could only make appointments on the advice of some designated institution or public official. Thus, the Chief Justice was appointed by the president on the advice of the Prime Minister and all other judges were appointed on the advice of the Judicial Service Commission. The vesting of formal appointment powers in a non-executive president was not without practical significance. The non-executive president was entitled to refuse a purely political appointment on the grounds of abuse of process. The fact that the Prime Minister was involved only in the appointment of the Chief Justice allowed the Judicial Service Commission to act with independence and professionalism.

Secondly, regarding the appointment of the Chief Justice, the Prime Minister was required i) to consult and consider the recommendations of the Judicial Service Commission before tendering his advice to the president; and ii) to inform Parliament 'before the appointment is made', where his advice differed from the recommendations of the Commission. The requirement to inform Parliament before an appointment meant that the president had to take into account the views of Parliament before accepting the Prime Minister's advice. It was competent, under this framework, for the president to decline the Prime Minister's proposed appointee on the grounds of disapproval by Parliament. This is the only reading that appears to give substance to the constitutional requirement that Parliament be informed 'before the appointment is made'.

Thirdly, it created a four-member Judicial Service Commission: the Chief Justice or the most senior judge of the Supreme Court; the Chairperson of the Public Service Commission; a highly experienced lawyer; and one other person. Given that the Chairperson of the Public Service Commission had to be a person who had held the post of Secretary or Deputy Secretary or Under-Secretary in a Ministry, the rationale of this composition was to have a professional commission which could not easily be manipulated by political considerations.

Qualifications for appointment as judges

It has already been said that:

> The setting of minimum qualifications for appointment restricts the degree of manoeuvre by those empowered to make judicial appointments, thereby contributing to an independent judiciary. In other words, as long as judges have to be appointed from a restricted class, the risk of purely political choices is reduced because either there may be fewer willing political tools within the restricted group or, generally, members of the restricted class may be bound by certain professional standards which militate against subscribing to a political superior at the expense of the law.[13]

To qualify for appointment as a judge in Zimbabwe, a person must satisfy one of the two minimum requirements set out by the Constitution. The first is having been a judge of a court of 'unlimited jurisdiction in civil or criminal matters in a country in which the common law is Roman Dutch or English and in which English is an official language'.[14] A court of 'unlimited jurisdiction' is a superior court at the level of the High Court. The second requirement is having been qualified to practice as a legal practitioner for not less than seven years in Zimbabwe or in a country in which the common law is Roman Dutch or, for a citizen of Zimbabwe, in a country in which the common law is English.[15]

Both requirements have inherent weaknesses. The first requirement does not prescribe any minimum period during which the person in question has held judicial office. A person would therefore qualify for appointment even where he/she has held judicial office for a short and inconsequential period. Further, the qualifications for appointment to judicial office in the country in question are irrelevant. This means that a person with fewer legal qualifications than those stipulated in Section 82 (1) (b) would qualify for appointment under Section 82 (1) (a) if he/she has held judicial office in a country that accepts his/her qualifications.

The second requirement is unclear in one respect. The stipulation of a minimum time period of qualification suggests that the intention is to limit appointment to persons who have gained adequate legal experience in practice. However, the expression 'qualified to practice' may be literally interpreted to mean that the person need not have been actively practicing for this time. As some recent appointments to the High Court indicate that this interpretation has been applied, this cannot easily be dismissed as an absurdity.

Although this problematic formulation has its origins in the Lancaster House document, the ambiguity relating to whether or not actual practice is required did not arise under the original provisions. As the Lancaster House document restricted the appointment of judges to advocates, attorneys were not eligible for appointment as judges. It is submitted that with advocates, unlike legal practitioners in general, it is difficult to describe a person as 'qualified to practise as an advocate' when he/she is not actually practising as such.

Compulsory retirement versus executive discretion to extend the term of office of a judge

In some jurisdictions, the executive has discretion to extend the term of office of a judge. Where such discretion is unlimited, it undermines the independence of the judiciary in that an extension may only be granted to those who are perceived to be 'good' judges. Tanzania offers a typical example. Section 110 (3) of the Tanzanian Constitution states that:

> In the event that the President considers it to be in the public interest that a judge who has attained sixty years of age continues in office and the judge agrees in writing to continue in office, then the President may direct that the judge continue in office for any period which may be specified by the President.

In order to avoid this avenue of executive influence over the judiciary, some jurisdictions that are determined to protect the independence of the judiciary provide for a compulsory retirement age that cannot be extended by the executive. In such jurisdictions, a judge who has reached retirement age may only remain in office for a limited period necessary to enable him/her to finish proceedings commenced before the attainment of the retirement age.[16]

In this area, Zimbabwe is in a unique position. The Constitution imposes a compulsory retirement age of 70 and the executive has no powers, in any circumstances whatsoever, to extend the term of office of a judge who has reached this age.[17] However, not every judge is entitled to remain in office until reaching this age. The Constitution imposes an early retirement age of 65 but allows a judge to elect not to retire but to serve up to the age of seventy.[18] The choice to continue to serve is subject to the involvement of the executive. The judge is required to submit a medical report on his/her mental and physical fitness to continue in office to the president. On receipt of the report, the president, after consulting the Judicial Service Commission, may either accept or reject the report. Only if the president accepts the medical report may the relevant judge serve beyond 65 years of age. Thus, if the president rejects the medical report, the judge must retire at 65. It has already been observed that the power of the president lies in either accepting or rejecting the medical report, but this is a limited form of power as it is unlikely that the president may reject an otherwise sound report merely to terminate a judge's tenure of office.[19]

Another avenue through which the executive may exert influence on individual judges is over the appointment of acting judges and judges for a fixed period. Section 84 (3) of the Constitution provides for the appointment of a judge for a fixed period, but there is no provision in the Constitution prohibiting the renewal of fixed term appointments. Renewal of a fixed-term contract provides an incentive for some judges to toe the line of the executive. For this reason, any Constitution that is anxious to preserve judicial independence will prohibit the renewal of fixed-term contracts. An example is Section 176 (1) of the South African Constitution that provides as follows:

> A Constitutional Court judge is appointed for a non-renewable term of 12 years, but must retire at the age of 70.

In Zimbabwe, acting judges are easy prey for the executive. In terms of Section 85 (2), the president is empowered to appoint an acting judge *inter alia* 'if the services of an additional judge of the High Court are required for a limited period'. A 'limited period' is not fully defined, nor is it clear as to the circumstances that may warrant the services of an additional judge. Further, it is the president who determines whether or not a given set of facts warrants the services of an additional judge and if so, the length of the limited period. The appointment of an acting judge may, in circumstances where the period of appointment is not specified, be revoked by the president at any time.[20] The weak constitutional protection of acting judges may influence the executive to use the institution of the acting judge to make purely political appointments for limited political objectives.

The removal of judges from office

Appointment to and removal from office are two sides of the same coin. If a judge can easily be removed from office, it matters very little that the appointment process is rigorous and free from political manipulation. If judges enjoy adequate security of tenure, it may offset the effects of a defective appointment system in that once appointed, a judge who knows that it is difficult to remove him/her from office may develop an independent line, regardless of the original motivations for his appointment.

International standards on the preservation of the independence of the judiciary place considerable emphasis against the improper removal of judges from office. They insist that a judge facing any risk of removal be judged by an independent and impartial tribunal and that the grounds for removal be limited to either the inability to perform judicial duties or serious misconduct.[21]

Zimbabwe's provisions on the removal of a judge from office demonstrate an admirable sensitivity to the need to protect judges from improper removal. First, a distinction is made between the Chief Justice and other judges. For the Chief Justice (the head of the judiciary), the process of his/her removal from office can only be initiated by the president.[22] For all other judges, the president – on the advice of the Chief Justice – must appoint a tribunal to investigate the question of removal from office.[23] In other words, without the approval of the Chief Justice, the president cannot initiate the process leading to the removal of a judge from office. In this way, the judiciary itself is placed at the centre of the removal process. The rationale of this approach is for the Chief Justice to advise the president only in circumstances where it is reasonable and justifiable for an investigation to be conducted. However, Section 87 (3) does not prohibit Parliament or the executive from raising the issue of the removal of a judge from office. Once the issue is raised, whether by Parliament or the executive, it must be referred to the Chief Justice, who has the sole power to decide whether or not to advise the president. If the Chief Justice declines to advise the president, that is the end of the matter.

Second, the investigations as to whether or not there is a basis for removal are conducted by a tribunal appointed by the president. The tribunal should consist of not less than three members selected from three categories of persons, namely (i) persons who have held office as a judge of the Supreme Court or High Court, (ii) persons who hold or have held high judicial office in a Roman Dutch or an English jurisdiction and (iii) legal practitioners of not less than seven years' standing nominated by the Law Society of Zimbabwe.[24]

One question that has arisen is whether or not the president may appoint all members of the tribunal from only one of the categories specified in Section 87 (4). It is submitted that from both a literal and purposive reading of Section 87 (4), it is acceptable for the president to appoint all members of the tribunal from only one of the categories. From a literal standpoint, the critical words are 'from the following'. These words clearly point to the fact that the various categories are in fact derived from one group. Further, although members of the tribunal must be no less than three in number, it is for the president to determine its actual size. Thus, where the president decides to appoint more than three members, it is clear that he is not limited to using multiples of three, so as to appoint an equal number from each category. This shows that each category merely contributes to one pool from which the president is required to select the tribunal. A purposive interpretation is that it is clear that the intention of Section 87 (4) is to restrict the appointment of members of the tribunal to those persons who qualify for appointment as judges. Thus, the various categories can be seen as merely an enunciation of the group of persons who qualify for appointment as judges in terms of Section 82. Accordingly, no purpose can be served by insisting that a choice be made from each category, since there is only one category of persons qualified for appointment as judges.

Third, the president is bound by the recommendations of the tribunal following its obligatory enquiry.[25] An enquiry necessarily means that the judge in question must be afforded an opportunity to present his/her side of the story. Instructively, the tribunal has only two options: it recommends either (i) that there is no basis for the removal of the judge, in which case the president must revoke his/her suspension, or (ii) that there is a basis for the removal of the judge from office, in which case the president must refer the matter to the Judicial Service Commission.[26] The tribunal only has a final say where it resolves that the judge not be removed from office. Removal from office is considered a serious matter and the Constitution requires that a recommendation of the tribunal to that effect is not in itself final. A second consideration must be made by the Judicial Service Commission. A judge can only be removed from office if, after considering the recommendations of the tribunal to that effect, the Judicial Service Commission advises the president to do so.[27] There is no provision stipulating that the Judicial Service Commission is bound by the recommendations of the tribunal. That the Judicial Service Commission may be against removal and recommend instead that the suspension be revoked is implied by the wording of Section 87 (8).

Fourth, as already stated, the grounds of removal are limited to the inability to perform the functions of judicial office arising from infirmity to body or mind or other cause and to misbehaviour.[28] Although 'misbehaviour' is not defined, it is submitted that it cannot be taken to cover the broad and vague ground of 'incompetence' found in other jurisdictions.

The Supreme Court has held that misbehaviour includes criminal misconduct.[29] In the words of Sandura JA:

> Although the Constitution does not say what constitutes misbehaviour, I have no doubt in my mind that it includes criminal misconduct. If that were not the case, there would be an obvious absurdity because it would mean that a judge could be removed from office for ethical transgressions but could not be removed from office if he committed a criminal offence, no matter how serious the offence may be. That could hardly have been the intention of the framers of the Constitution.[30]

This has raised a critical issue: If a judge is alleged to have committed a criminal offence and it being the position that that constitutes misbehaviour in terms of Section 87, is it competent for the criminal authorities to arrest and prosecute that judge before proceedings under Section 87 have been initiated and completed? This was the crux of the matter in *Benjamin Paradza v The Minister of Justice, Legal and Parliamentary Affairs*.[31] In this case, the applicant was a judge of the High Court. He had been arrested on allegations of committing the offence of obstructing the course of justice. It had been alleged that he had corruptly attempted to influence the decision of two other judges who were presiding over a case involving his business partner. After his arrest, he was detained in custody for one night, after which he was taken to the Magistrates Court for an initial appearance. He was remanded out of custody on bail. He then lodged an application in the Supreme Court challenging the constitutionality of his arrest and detention. He argued, *inter alia*, that his arrest contravened Section 87 of the Constitution in that as a judge he had a right to be dealt with in terms of that Section before any criminal proceedings could be instituted against him. In other words, a judge who is alleged to have committed a criminal offence cannot be arrested and prosecuted before Section 87 has been invoked. Malaba JA summarized the applicant's case as follows:

> The contention advanced by the applicant was that under the constitutional scheme, criminal proceedings cannot be instituted against a sitting judge of the Supreme Court or High Court before the procedure provided for in Section 87 of the Constitution for his removal from office has been gone into

and completed, because to do so would violate the principle of judicial independence contained in Section 79B. He argued that the initiation of criminal proceedings against him before the procedure for his removal from office had been gone into and completed should be declared unconstitutional. He did not claim that a judge of the Supreme Court or High Court enjoyed immunity from prosecution for criminal offences.[32]

By a majority of four to one, the Supreme Court rejected this contention. Malaba JA, who delivered the majority judgment, had a two-pronged basis for his conclusions. First, the applicant's contention, in according primacy to the procedure for the removal of a judge from office for criminal misconduct over the institution of criminal proceedings, involved an interpretation of Section 87 as violating Section 76 (4) (a), which gives the Attorney General exclusive jurisdiction to institute criminal proceedings.

Secondly, he rejected the contention that the institution of criminal proceedings before initiating the procedure for removal violated the principle of judicial independence protected by Section 79B. He held that Section 79B only covers the individual independence of a judge when he/she is discharging adjudicating functions. A judge cannot be said to be exercising judicial authority at the time he/she commits a criminal offence and is therefore not protected by the principle of judicial independence.

In his minority judgment, Sandura JA adopted what he claimed to be a 'generous and purposive' approach to constitutional interpretation. He held that the arrest and detention of the applicant contravened Section 79B in that it (the arrest and detention) placed him under the control of persons who are not members of the judiciary. In his view, in terms of Section 79B, a judge, 'whilst serving as such, cannot be placed under the factual direction or control of anyone other than that of another member of the judiciary in terms of a written law'.[33] Regarding Section 87, and applying his 'generous and purposive interpretation', Sandura JA reasoned that the framers of the Constitution must have intended that the elaborate procedures for the removal of a judge from office be invoked before any criminal proceedings could commence. He expressed his view thus:

> In my view, it could not have been the intention of the framers of the Constitution that a police officer could arrest a judge and trigger the prosecution, indictment and trial of the judge before the Chief Justice has had an opportunity to consider whether to advise the president that the question of the judge's removal from office should be investigated. They must have intended that the allegations would first be investigated and the facts ascertained by a high-powered judicial tribunal consisting of judges, former judges and law-

yers qualified for appointment as judges before the police are involved in the investigations.[34]

It is submitted that a proper analysis of the Constitution supports the result reached by the majority. However, the reasoning of both the majority and minority on Section 87 was weak and simplistic. It is difficult to understand how the majority could bring in the issue of the independence of the Attorney General when it is clear that he/she must exercise his/her authority in accordance with the Constitution. The sole issue was the proper meaning of Section 87. If it were to be established, on a proper interpretation, that this required the initiation of removal proceedings before any criminal proceedings, a declaration of that meaning by the Supreme Court would not have placed the court in a position of directing the actions of the Attorney General. The court would have been merely involved in discharging its duty of determining what the Constitution means and the Attorney General would have then been bound by that meaning.

Section 87 does not compel the removal from office of every judge who has become unable to discharge the functions of his office or who is guilty of misbehaviour. Its purpose is to promote judicial independence by protecting judges from improper removal.

It is clear from Sections 87 (2) and (3) that the tribunal is not necessarily required to investigate the misbehaviour or the inability to discharge the functions of judicial office, but whether or not the circumstances thereof warrant removal from office. In other words, misbehaviour may be established independent of the process in which the tribunal is involved, but the latter is involved in determining whether the scope of that misbehaviour warrants removal from office. Thus, with criminal misconduct, it is clear that no person can be said to be guilty of criminal misconduct until they have been convicted by a criminal court. Misbehaviour, with respect to criminal misconduct, only arises when a person has been convicted of a criminal offence.

The scheme of the Constitution is therefore that a judge accused of committing a criminal offence must be subjected to due process. If he/she is convicted, that constitutes criminal misconduct and, *prima facie*, misbehaviour within the contemplation of the Constitution. It is at that point that a tribunal may be appointed to determine whether or not the scope of that misbehaviour warrants removal from office.

This approach is consistent with other values protected by the Constitution, such as equality before the law and presumption of innocence. The fact that only the president is given immunity from criminal prosecution while in office shows that all other persons may be subjected to criminal prosecution without any preconditions and regardless of their station in life.[35]

In a properly functioning democracy, which is what the framers of the Constitution had in mind, the arrest, detention and prosecution of a judge in accordance with the due process of the law does not pose any threat to the independence of the judiciary. If anything, it promotes an open and free society founded on equality before the law.

Sandura JA referred to what he termed an 'absurdity' in a situation where a judge who is prosecuted before removal proceedings may continue to sit as a judge while the criminal prosecution is in progress. This situation is catered for by Section 87, which is sufficiently wide to allow the initiation of the investigation of the question of removal from office before the completion of the criminal prosecution. The tribunal appointed under Section 87 may wait for the completion of the criminal prosecution, but the suspension of the judge would have been achieved under Section 87 (8).

Unproven allegations, while not constituting criminal misconduct, may be such that they point to unethical conduct. In appropriate cases, unethical conduct may constitute misbehaviour in terms of Section 87. Where allegations of criminal misconduct are made against a judge, three scenarios arise. First, the criminal authorities may initiate their processes, in which case they may investigate, arrest, detain and prosecute the judge. Section 87 does not prohibit this course of action, nor does it set any preconditions.

Secondly, where criminal processes have commenced, the responsible authorities (the president and/or the Chief Justice) may wait for the final outcome before embarking on the procedure set out in Section 87. However, under this scenario, the outcome of the criminal process may or may not affect this procedure. For example, the acquittal of a judge may be the basis for dismissing any charges of misbehaviour. However, an acquittal may not prevent the institution of the Section 87 procedure. The circumstances surrounding the allegations may still amount to such conduct as may be regarded as misbehaviour for purposes of Section 87 (1). In this case, the authorities may invoke the procedure in Section 87 as if they were proceeding in accordance with the third scenario.

The authorities may invoke Section 87 as soon as the allegations of criminal misconduct arise, regardless of whether the criminal authorities do anything about it. Under this third scenario, the alleged criminal misconduct need not be established as a criminal offence, but only as evidence of misbehaviour. Under this scenario, whether or not the judge has been arrested and prosecuted is irrelevant. Whether or not he/she was convicted following prosecution is also irrelevant. The sole issue of importance is to determine whether the allegations may lead to a finding of misbehaviour.

Regarding Section 79B and *Benjamin Paradza v The Minister of Justice, Legal and Parliamentary Affairs*, it is submitted that the view of the majority was correct. The Constitution does not place judges in a class of their own, but rather protects the independence of the judiciary as an institution. While this necessarily requires that individual judges be protected from unlawful harassment, it cannot be used to shield individual judges from the consequences of criminal conduct. It is contrary to the rule of law to create a society in which some persons are not subject to the ordinary process of law if they commit criminal offences.

The suggestion by Sandura JA that a judge who has been arrested has been placed under the 'control or direction' of another person contrary to Section 79B cannot be supported. As Section 79B opens with the words 'in the exercise of his judicial authority', the 'control' to which it refers to is in respect of the discharge of the functions of the judicial office.

Other features on the independence of the judiciary
Provision on judicial independence

Section 79B of the Constitution is very clear on the independence of the judiciary, stating that:

> In the exercise of his judicial authority, a member of the judiciary shall not be subject to the direction or control of any person or authority, except to the extent that a written law may place him under the direction or control of another member of the judiciary.

Such a statement has both legal and political value. In political terms, it provides a basis for political actors to criticize and mobilize against any tendencies of the executive to interfere with the work of the judiciary. Such criticism and mobilization may have a restraining impact on the executive. In legal terms, it allows redress to be sought in the courts in the event of a law or action undermining the independence of the judiciary. A case in point is *Benjamin Paradza v The Minister of Justice, Legal and Parliamentary Affairs*, where the applicant approached the Supreme

Court contending that his arrest and detention were unconstitutional as they infringed Sections 79B and 87 of the Constitution.[36] Although the majority of the court dismissed the contention on the grounds that the particular circumstances of the case did not support the argument, the entire court accepted the premise that a legal action can be mounted on the basis of Section 79B.

Section 79B has two weaknesses. First is the position allowing a member of the judiciary to be placed under the control or direction of another. In principle, this is unacceptable: a judge must also be independent from his/her colleagues on the bench. It is not unusual for some members of Zimbabwe's senior judiciary to be 'amenable' to political and other pressures. To allow such elements to control their juniors constitutes a serious threat to the independence of the judiciary. It is for this reason that in other countries the formulation favoured is that the courts are subject 'only to the Constitution and the law'.[37]

Secondly, it does not go further to provide for a positive duty on other organs of the state to promote the independence of the judiciary. An example of such a provision is Article 78 (3) of the Namibian Constitution, which provides that:

> All organs of the state shall accord such assistance as the courts may require to protect their independence, dignity and effectiveness, subject to the terms of this Constitution or any other law.[38]

Vesting judicial functions exclusively in the Judiciary

In order to protect the independence of the judiciary, the Constitution must prevent the executive and/or legislature from sidestepping the judiciary by assigning some judicial functions to bodies other than the courts. Malawi's Constitution offers a classic example of how this may be achieved. It states that:

> The judiciary shall have jurisdiction over all issues of a judicial nature and shall have exclusive authority to decide whether an issue is within its competence.[39]

Zimbabwe's Constitution has a frightening provision that allows the state to avoid the judiciary under ill-defined circumstances. Section 79 provides as follows:

> (1) The judicial authority of Zimbabwe shall vest in:
> the Supreme Court, and
> the High Court, and

such other courts subordinate to the Supreme Court and the High Court as may be established by or under an Act of Parliament.

(2) The provisions of sub-Section (1) shall not be construed as preventing an Act of Parliament from:

vesting adjudicating functions in a person or authority other than a court referred to in sub-Section (1), or

vesting functions other than adjudicating functions in a court referred to in sub-Section (1) or in a member of the judiciary.

Sub-Section (2), which provides the basis for avoiding the judiciary, was brought about by Constitution of Zimbabwe Amendment 11 with the deliberate intention of side-stepping the courts in the event of them resisting the land reform process.[40] Unfortunately, the clause has become a permanent feature of the Constitution and a fertile ground for abuse. Recent developments confirm a trend where some adjudicating functions in politically sensitive areas are being placed in the hands of partisan bodies. For example, Section 25 (5) of the notorious Public Order and Security Act renders the Minister of Home Affairs himself an appeal court against decisions made by a regulating authority.[41] It says:

> Any person who is aggrieved by a direction issued under sub-Section (1) may appeal against it to the Minister, and the Minister may confirm, vary or set aside the direction in the matter as he thinks just.[42]

Another example is the Access to Information and Protection of Privacy Act, which gives extensive powers of review to the Media Commission that amount to the exercise of adjudicating functions.[43]

Notes

1. See Bailey and Gunn (1996), p. 113.
2. Ibid., p. 113-11.
3. Legal Practitioners (exemption from professional examinations) University of Zimbabwe – Notice, 1994 (SI 49 of 1994).
4. See Section 7 of Legal Practitioners (Council for Legal Education) Rules, 1992 (SI 447 of 1992).
5. Ibid. See the Schedule.
6. 1995 (1) *ZLR* 235 (S), 244E.
7. See Section 28 of the Legal Practitioners Act.
8. Ibid., Section 32.
9. See L. Madhuku (2002) 'Constitutional Protection of the Independence of the Judiciary: A Survey of the position in Southern Africa', *Journal of African Law* (46), 232: p. 234.

10. See Section 84 (2) of the Constitution of Zimbabwe.
11. Ibid., see Section 90.
12. For a comparative survey of the compositions of Judiciary Service Commissions in Southern Africa, see Madhuku (2002), pp. 238-9.
13. Ibid., p. 241.
14. See Section 82 (1) (a).
15. See Section 82 (1) (b).
16. See, for example, Section 145 (Ghana); Section 97 (Botswana); Section 144 (Uganda); Section 62 (Kenya); Section 121 (Lesotho); Section 119 (Malawi).
17. See Section 86 (1).
18. Ibid.
19. See Madhuku (2002), p. 243.
20. See Section 85 (3) (a).
21. See Latimer House Guidelines, p. 7.
22. See Section 87 (2) of the Constitution of Zimbabwe.
23. Ibid., Section 87 (3).
24. Ibid., Section 87 (4).
25. Ibid., Section 87 (6).
26. Ibid.
27. Ibid., Section 87 (9).
28. Ibid., Section 87 (1).
29. See *Benjamin Paradza v The Minister of Justice, Legal and Parliamentary Affairs v Others* SC 46/03.
30. Ibid. pp. 11, 30. Malaba JA, who delivered the majority judgment, was in agreement on this point.
31. *Benjamin Paradza v The Minister of Justice, Legal and Parliamentary Affairs v Others* SC 46/03SC 46/03.
32. Ibid., p. 27.
33. Ibid., p. 10.
34. Ibid., p. 17.
35. For Presidential immunity, see Section 30 of the Constitution of Zimbabwe.
36. Ibid.
37. See, for example, Section 165 (2) of the South African Constitution and Article 78 (2) of the Namibian Constitution.
38. See also Section 118 (3) of the Lesotho Constitution; Section 165 (4) of the South African Constitution; Section 127 (2) of the Ghanaian Constitution; and Section 128 (3) of the Ugandan Constitution.
39. See Section 103 (2) of the Malawian Constitution, 1994. See also Section 125 (3) of the Ghanaian Constitution.
40. See Section 10 of Act No. 30 of 1990.
41. Public Order and Security Act, Chapter 11:17.
42. Ibid., Section 26 (4).
43. Ibid. Chapter 10:27. See also, for example, Sections 53-7.

7

An Outline of Court Procedures

Civil Procedures

Adversarial versus inquisitorial procedure

A distinction should be made between *adversarial* and *inquisitorial* procedure. Their difference boils down to the extent of participation of the court/judge in the proceedings. An inquisitorial procedure is one in which the judge takes an active role in ascertaining the facts from the parties, going so far as to do a great deal of questioning of witnesses, deciding which witnesses are to be called and determining the manner in which the trial is to proceed.

The adversarial procedure is one in which the court is merely an impartial umpire or referee, leaving the proceedings entirely in the hands of the parties. The system is based on the thesis that there are two adversaries in every dispute: one contending for one thing and the other rejecting it. The court only interferes in the proceedings to enforce the rules of evidence and procedure; otherwise its duty is to decide at the end, which of the two sides has been successful. The non-intervention of the judge in the adversarial system is more pronounced in a criminal trial. The role of the judge in a civil trial under the adversarial system was expressed by Denning LJ in *Jones v National Coal Board* [1957] 2 Q.B 55 in the following terms:

> The judge's part ... is to hearken to the evidence, only himself asking ... witnesses when it is necessary to clear up any point that has been overlooked or left obscure; to see that the advocates behave themselves seemly and keep to the rules laid down by law; to exclude irrelevancies and discourage repetition;

to make sure by wise intervention that he follows the points that the advocates are making and can assess their work; and at the end to make up his mind where the truth lies.[1]

Civil trial procedure versus application procedure

There are two ways of pursuing a civil suit: a *trial* procedure and an *application* procedure. The law may specify, in a given situation, which procedure is applicable. In the absence of a specific direction by law, the choice between the two depends on whether or not there are any material disputes of facts. The trial procedure must be followed whenever there are material disputes of fact. This procedure is called 'trial' because it involves the court in making a finding of fact between two versions of facts. The *application* procedure is used where there are no material disputes of facts, with the issue restricted only to disputes of law. The court itself is called upon to make a determination of the law applicable. In an application, facts are addressed by way of affidavits, and where disputes arise, the court resolves them on the papers.

Civil trial procedure

There are differences in the civil trial procedures of the High Court and the Magistrates Court. This section deals with those procedures common to both courts, but references may be given where appropriate to the differences. In both courts, procedures are governed by *Rules of Court*.

Letter of Demand

Most civil claims are commenced by a *letter of demand*, whereby the plaintiff makes a claim from the defendant, warning that if it is not settled within a specified time, he/she will institute civil proceedings. Except for claims where the parties have agreed on a demand as a condition precedent to instituting civil action, a letter of demand is not a legal requirement.

Issue of Summons

A civil trial action in both the Magistrates Court and the High Court is commenced by the issue of a summons. A summons calls upon the defendant to answer the plaintiff's claim within a specified period of time.

AN OUTLINE OF COURT PROCEDURES

The period within which the defendant must answer the claim is called the *dies induciae*. In a Magistrates Court, the summons must contain *particulars of claim*, setting out the cause of action. In the High Court, the particulars setting out the plaintiff's case – which are usually attached to the summons – are contained in what is called the *Declaration*.

In both courts, the summons can *only* be served on the other party by a court official. In the Magistrates Court, it is by the *Messenger of Court*, while in the High Court, it is by the *Sheriff* or *Deputy Sheriff*. Before a summons can be served, it must be *issued* by the court, i.e., signed and stamped by the clerk of court (for the Magistrates Court) and Registrar (for the High Court).

Appearance to defend

Where the defendant wishes to defend the action, he/she should 'enter an appearance to defend'. This must be in the form of a written statement filed with the court. Where the defendant does not wish to defend the action, he/she may *consent* to judgment. Where he/she fails to enter an appearance to defend altogether, the plaintiff may obtain *default* judgment. Where the plaintiff is convinced that the defendant has no *bona fide* defence to the claim and has only entered appearance to buy time, the plaintiff may apply to court for what is called *summary judgment*.

Request for further particulars

After entering an appearance to defend, the defendant may request further particulars from the plaintiff to enable him/her to *plead* (i.e., answer the plaintiff's claim).

Defendant's plea

This is the defendant's answer to the plaintiff's claim. It must first be *filed* with the court and then served on the plaintiff. It must be filed within the times specified in the Rules of Court. In addition to a plea, the defendant may make a *counter claim* (making a claim against the plaintiff).

Request for further particulars

The plaintiff may require the defendant to furnish particulars to enable him/her to reply.

AN OUTLINE OF COURT PROCEDURES

Replication

This is the plaintiff's reply to the defendant's plea. This is normally necessary where the defendant makes certain allegations in the plea that require a response.

Close of pleadings

The above documents from the summons to the replication are technically called *pleadings*. They are deemed closed if the parties join the issue, i.e., make it clear that they are in disagreement and look to a trial for resolution of the dispute.

Discovery

After close of pleadings, either party may apply for *discovery*, i.e., requiring the other party to specify the documents and books which he/she intends to use at the trial. Books and/or documents not disclosed may not be used at the trial by the party who failed to disclose them.

Pre-trial conference

After discovery, a pre-trial conference is held. This is attended by both parties and chaired by a judge or magistrate, as the case may be. The purpose of a pre-trial conference is to define the issues and reach agreement, where possible, on issues such as the length of trial, the number of witnesses, and exhibits. Another purpose of the conference is to explore the possibility of settling the matter without going to trial.

Trial date

In the High Court, a trial date may be obtained at the pre-trial conference. If not, an application for a date has to be made. In the Magistrates Court, a trial date is obtained from the clerk of court. After getting a date, the party who obtained it must file and serve a notice of *set-down*.

The trial

The issue to note here is that the burden of proof is on the plaintiff. In order to succeed, he/she must prove his/her case on a *balance of probabilities*.

Judgment

The court will give judgment at the end of the trial. A judgment may take one of three forms: i) judgment for the plaintiff; ii) judgment for the defendant; or iii) *absolution from the instance*. Absolution from the instance means that neither party has won the case and the parties remain where they were before the trial started.

Enforcement of judgment

A civil judgment may be enforced by any one of the following methods:

Execution of property

A warrant/writ of execution may be issued against both movable and immovable property. Immovable property may only be attached if there is insufficient movable property to satisfy the judgment. Certain property that is essential to sustain life and work for the judgment debtor and his/her family may not be attached. This includes clothing, food, professional books/documents and tools of trade. Execution of property to satisfy a judgment of a Magistrates Court is carried out by the messenger of court, while for a judgment of the High Court, it is the Sheriff or Deputy Sheriff.

Garnishee order

This order may be made against any debt due or to become due to the judgment debtor. It is usually against salaries or wages, and in such a case, the garnishee order requires the employer (the garnishee) to pay a portion of the wages every month to the judgment creditor until the judgment debt has been paid off. It is a requirement of the law that in determining the portion of the salaries or wages to be deducted under a garnishee order, the amount left over after the deduction must be sufficient to enable the judgment debtor to maintain himself/herself and his/her dependents.

Civil imprisonment

This means imprisoning a debtor as a means of compelling him/her to satisfy the judgment. It is not a punishment for a debtor who has no financial means to pay. Accordingly, civil imprisonment is only available where it is proven that the debtor has the ability to pay and that his/her failure is wilful. The maximum period of civil imprisonment is three months, but a debtor must be immediately released if the debt is paid before the three months have elapsed. Where a debtor serves the full imprisonment for the debt, he/she may not be re-imprisoned for the same debt, but the judgment debt is not discharged. The latter situation means that the other methods of enforcement such as execution of property and a garnishee order may still be utilized. The Supreme Court gave a useful summary of the scope of civil imprisonment in *Chinamora v Angwa Furnishers (Pvt.) Ltd*:

> Civil imprisonment is a method of execution in respect of civil debts and is employed to obtain satisfaction of a judgment sounding in money. It is a procedure that has been available and operating in this country since just before the turn of the century. It involves the imprisonment of the debtor, at the instance of the creditor, in a public gaol for a fixed period or until, before the expiration of that period he has paid the debt owing by him, or until he is otherwise legally discharged. It is intended as a means of compelling a debtor, who is able to do so, to satisfy a judgment. It is not a measure for punishing a debtor who cannot pay. The cost of maintaining the debtor in prison is borne by the creditor and not by the state.[2]

The Supreme Court holds that civil imprisonment is not unconstitutional and has rejected arguments that civil imprisonment is contrary to Sections 13 (1) and 15 (1) of the Declaration of Rights in the Constitution of Zimbabwe.[3]

Contempt of court

A leading textbook has a very illuminating passage on contempt of court in the following words:

> Contempt of court can assume various forms. The main division is that between criminal and civil contempt of court. Criminal contempt may be constituted by conduct which is disrespectful to the court, such as wilful insult to the court or the interruption of court proceedings or other conduct of that nature amounting to misbehaviour, and is punishable at common law. Civil contempt, on the other hand, is the wilful and *mala fide* [bad faith] refusal or failure to comply with an order of court. Committal to gaol for civil contempt of court is a mode of procedure aimed at enforcing civil orders of court, and to bring to its logical conclusion an order given by a judge which the court finds has been deliberately disobeyed.[4]

Civil contempt of court proceedings are designed to compel performance of the court order through the device of committing the defaulting party to prison. The imprisonment imposed is, in most cases, suspended pending performance by the defaulting party. Contempt of court becomes a way of enforcement of judgment in that the person seeking compliance with the order applies to court to have the defaulter found guilty of, and to be subsequently jailed for, contempt of court. The imprisonment of the court is thus utilized as a way of exerting pressure for compliance with the court order. The defaulting party can avoid imprisonment simply by complying with the court order.

In order to hold a person in contempt of court, two requirements must be satisfied, namely, that:

1. The order was not complied with.
2. Non-compliance was wilful on the part of the defaulting party.[5]

Once it is proven that the order has not been complied with, there is a rebuttable inference that the non-compliance was wilful. The onus is thus on the defaulting party to rebut the inference on a balance of probabilities.[6]

The difference in purpose between civil imprisonment and imprisonment for contempt of court leads to an important consequence regarding the period of committal to prison. Whereas with civil imprisonment, a person cannot be imprisoned more that once for the same failure to pay a debt, imprisonment for contempt can be repeated for the same contempt as long as non-compliance with the court order continues.[7]

Appeals & reviews

A person dissatisfied with a judgment of the court may appeal to a higher court. Here, it is necessary to distinguish an appeal from a review. An appeal is concerned with the *merits* of the decision appealed against, i.e., whether it was right or wrong, while a *review* is concerned with the decision-making process (the procedure followed). Mary Welsh (1996) offers an instructive set of differences between reviews and appeals:

1. An appeal is based on the argument that the method used to arrive at the decision was wrong.
2. In an appeal the parties are bound by the record. In a review, the irregularity may not appear from the record and the applicant may have to prove facts outside the record.
3. An appeal may be brought solely at the instance of the parties. Other interested persons may apply for a review.
4. An appeal is limited to the final stages of an action while a review may

AN OUTLINE OF COURT PROCEDURES

be brought at any stage of the proceedings.

5. The procedure for appeals and reviews differs.[8]

There is no automatic right of appeal. An appeal is only available if granted by statute. Some statutes go so far as to put matters beyond doubt by stipulating that certain decisions and/or judgments are not subject to appeal. Where a statute provides for a right to appeal, the scope of the appeal must be within the four 'corners' of the statute. For instance, the Labour Act (Chapter 28:01) provides that appeals from decisions of the Labour Court to the Supreme Court only lie in respect of questions of law.[9] In this regard, appeals in respect of questions of fact are not permissible.

The power of review vests in the High Court.[10] Except where it is prohibited by statute, a review is always available as long as the permissible grounds of review exist. The main grounds for a review arise when the decision sought to be reviewed is either:

1. Grossly unreasonable, or
2. Illegal, or
3. Was arrived at contrary to the principles of natural justice, or
4. Was made by a body that either lacked the jurisdiction to do so or exceeded its powers, i.e., acting *ultra vires*.

In an appeal, the appellant court may either affirm or set aside the decision appealed against. In respect of the latter situation, it is entitled to substitute its own decision for the one under appeal. In a review, the reviewing court may either set aside or refuse to dismiss the decision/proceedings. Where it sets aside the decision or proceedings, it is not entitled, except in exceptional circumstances, to substitute its own decision. The proper approach is for it to remit the matter to the relevant body for a decision.

Application procedure

The steps in the application procedure are as follows:

1. *Application plus applicant's founding affidavit.*
   The application must be supported by a founding affidavit that presents the facts upon which the application is based. It must also indicate the order sought, for which a draft must be provided.

2. *Opposition plus respondent's opposing affidavit.*
   The respondent must state the fact of his/her opposition to the application and support it with an opposing affidavit. The opposing affidavit must

respond to each and every averment made in the founding affidavit, stating whether or not facts in the applicant's founding affidavit are being admitted or denied.

3. *Applicant's answering affidavit.*
The applicant may file a further affidavit that answers issues raised by the respondent, with particular focus on facts disputed by the latter. Any failure to challenge the respondent's version of the facts may be taken as an acceptance of that version.

4. *Heads of argument.*
These are written legal arguments supported by legal authorities. They must be filed with the court before the oral arguments given at the hearing.

5. *Hearing to present oral arguments.*
A hearing is either held in open court or in the judges' chambers to enable the parties to present oral arguments, if they so wish. The hearing may merely be utilized for the purpose of clarifying points made in the heads of argument.

6. *Judgment.*
The application is either dismissed or granted.

Criminal Procedure

General

Criminal prosecutions are principally undertaken in the name of the state, hence the description *S v X* or 'the State versus ...'. The prosecution is undertaken by a public official who is either the Attorney General or his/her representative. The decision as to whether or not to prosecute rests with the Attorney General and is not subject to interference from any other person.[11] The Attorney General will consider a variety of factors in determining whether or not to prosecute. These include sufficiency of evidence, choice of offence to charge, and immunity of the accused – the president, for example, cannot be charged.[12] Certain diplomats are also immune from prosecution.[13]

In the Magistrates Courts, prosecutions are conducted by public prosecutors who represent the Attorney General. The normal method of appointment is by a document signed by the Attorney General appointing the individual named as a public prosecutor for a particular magisterial province or regional division. A public prosecutor need not be a registered legal practitioner. However, a public prosecutor who is not a registered legal practitioner is expected to conduct herself/himself in accordance with the ethics of the legal profession. Accordingly, the role of a public prosecutor is not to secure a conviction at all costs but to assist the court in arriving at the correct verdict, while at the same time remaining an advocate for the state. Prosecutions in the High Court are usually conducted by law officers from the Attorney General's office who are registered legal practitioners. However, the Attorney General has the power to appoint any person to represent the state in the High Court.

A prosecution may be undertaken by a private person in certain limited circumstances. The private person is required to show some substantial and 'peculiar' interest (i.e., an interest different from that of any other member of the public) in the issue of the trial arising from some injury that the he/she has suffered as a consequence of the committing of the offence.[14] A private prosecutor must first obtain from the Attorney General a signed certificate in which the Attorney General declines to prosecute (*nolle prosequi*). The Attorney General may take over a private prosecution at any stage of the proceedings and the court has no discretion to refuse to grant such an order.[15] It is not easy to satisfy the requirements for a private prosecution. For instance, the injury suffered must be more than is suffered by society generally. In *Levy v Benatar*, the appellant had obtained a court order restraining the respondent from having contact with his daughter. When the respondent flouted that order, the appellant sought to bring a private prosecution for contempt of court. It was held that the offence had not caused him any injury that was not shared with other right-thinking members of society.[16]

Securing the presence of the accused

Criminal proceedings are preceded by securing the presence of the accused. There are three main methods of securing the presence of the accused, namely, arrest, summons and extradition.

An arrest may be carried out with or without a warrant and the circumstances of each are set out in the Criminal Procedure and Evidence Act.[17] A private person is also entitled to arrest in matters involving 'First Schedule' offences.[18] An arrested person must be brought before a police station as soon as possible and may only be detained at the police station for up to 48 hours before being brought to court. The 48-hour period may end up being longer where (i) it expires on a day which is not a court day or (ii) expires after 4 p.m. on a court day. In both cases, it is deemed to expire at 4 p.m. on the next court day. Even where it would effectively expire before 4 p.m. on a court day, the 48-hour period is extended to 4 p.m. on that court day. If detention is sought beyond the initial 48-hour period, the police must obtain a warrant for further detention from a judge or magistrate.[19]

The issue of a summons to appear in court is initiated by the public prosecutor. It is issued by the clerk of court and served by a messenger of court.

Extradition is the return of a suspected offender or a fugitive criminal from the country where he/she is found to the country where he/she is to be tried or has already been convicted. It may be effected through bilateral or multi-lateral agreements among countries or through ad hoc arrangements between any two countries. The relevant legislation in Zimbabwe is the Extradition Act (Chapter 9:08).

Bail

Where a person has been arrested and detained pending trial, he/she may be released on bail. Bail may also be granted after conviction pending appeal. As regards bail pending trial, the police may grant bail in respect of offences not listed in the Third Schedule (treason, sedition, murder, rape, robbery, etc.), but the granting officer must either be in charge of a police station or above the rank of Assistant Inspector.[20] A magistrate may grant bail in respect of any offence except those in the Third Schedule and in the Eighth Schedule. Bail for offences listed in the Third Schedule requires the consent of the Attorney General and for those in the Eighth Schedule bail has to be sought from the High Court. Although Section 13 (2) of the Constitution protects the right to personal liberty, the granting or refusal of bail by the courts is constitutionally recognized.[21] The main factors taken into account are (i) the likelihood that the accused will abscond; (ii) the likelihood of interference with witnesses or evidence; and (iii) the likelihood that the accused will commit another offence. Where bail is sought pending an appeal, different principles apply because the accused has been convicted and the presumption of innocence rebutted. Two main factors are considered, namely, (i) the likelihood that the accused will abscond, and ii) the prospects of success on appeal.

The trial process

The onus of proof in a criminal case is on the state, which is required to prove all the elements of the offence 'beyond reasonable doubt'. As already indicated in Chapter 3, this does not mean proof 'beyond a shadow of doubt'. In some cases, the onus may fall on the accused (for example, where the statute presumes certain facts adverse to the accused). However, in such cases, the onus is discharged merely on a 'balance of probabilities.'

The Attorney General or a public prosecutor may withdraw charges at any time before plea, but he/she may re-institute proceedings at a later stage. However, once the accused has pleaded, he/she is entitled to be either acquitted or found guilty.[22] Should the Attorney General withdraw charges after plea, the accused is entitled to a verdict of acquittal.

In the normal course of events, every criminal trial takes place in open court in the presence of the accused.[23] However, a trial in the absence of the accused may be permitted (i) where he/she so conducts himself/herself as to make it impracticable to continue in his/her presence or (ii) where the accused has been summoned to appear for trial on a charge whose prescribed penalty is a fine and only in default, imprisonment.[24] However, both (i) and (ii) seem to fall foul of Section 18 (3) of the Constitution, which sanctions trials in the accused's absence only when he/she has given his/her consent.

Stages of the trial process

The accused's entering of plea

A plea is the accused's answer to the charge. When the charge is put to the accused, he/she must enter a plea immediately. The normal procedure is for the accused to plead personally, even where he/she is represented by a legal practitioner. The two main pleas are 'Guilty' and 'Not Guilty'. Other pleas may also be entered. The accused may plead that he/she has already been acquitted of the offence (*autrefois acquit*) or that he/she has already been convicted of the offence (*autrefois convict*). If any such plea is established, the prosecution is stopped and the trial ended.

There are two further pleas, namely, (a) lack of jurisdiction of the court and (b) a Presidential pardon. If it is established that the court has no jurisdiction to conduct the trial, it cannot proceed and the trial is stopped. The granting of a presidential pardon in terms of the Constitution also has the effect of terminating the proceedings.[25]

There are circumstances where it is permissible for an accused person to apply to court, before or after conviction, for his/her plea to be altered from guilty to not guilty. All that is required is for the accused to offer a reasonable explanation for having pleaded guilty in the first instance.

Outline of the State's case

The prosecutor addresses the court on the nature of the state case and the material facts on which it is based. The recommended approach is to outline the evidence of each state witness and setting out the order in which the state proposes to lead its evidence.

Outline of the defence

This is only necessary for a trial in a Magistrates Court. In the High Court, the normal practice is for the accused to supply the Attorney General with a written outline of his/her defence before the opening of the trial in court. In a Magistrates Court, this outline must be given after the state's outline and before the leading of the evidence of the state. In it, the accused is expected to outline the nature of his/her defence and the material facts on which it is based. If the accused fails, at this stage, to mention a fact he/she could reasonably be expected to have mentioned, an adverse inference may be drawn against him. This means that such failure may be taken as tending to support evidence against him/her.

Evidence-in-chief

This involves the prosecutor leading evidence from state witnesses. It is the prosecutor's discretion to choose which witnesses to call to support the state's case. In general, witnesses are expected to adhere to the statement he/she made to the police. If there are material variations, the prosecutor is obliged to disclose them to the court. This does not change the legal position that statements made by the witness to the police are privileged.

Cross-examination

The purpose of cross-examination is to extract from the witness that which may discredit his/her evidence or otherwise reduce its value. This is done by questioning the witness. Except where the accused person is not legally represented, the failure to cross-examine a witness is, in general, taken as acceptance of the witness's evidence. Even where the accused is not represented, the failure to cross-examine a witness on material points inescapably leads to the drawing of adverse inference against the accused.

Re-examination

This involves the prosecutor putting questions to the witness in order to reinforce his/her evidence on points where the cross-examination may have watered it down. The re-examination must only deal with matters arising from the cross-examination. It cannot be used to elicit evidence that was not raised during examination-in-chief.

Closing of the State case

After the prosecutor has led evidence from all the state witnesses, the state case is closed.

Application for discharge of the accused at the close of the state case (optional)

At the close of the state case, the court has discretion to return a verdict of not guilty and discharge the accused person if:

(i) There is no evidence to prove an essential element of the offence.

Or:

(ii) Given the evidence led, no reasonable court might convict.

Or:

(iii) The evidence avaible is so manifestly unreliable that no reasonable court could safely act on it.[26]

The latter may be made pursuant to an application made by the accused or the court may act on its own accord (*ex mero motu*).

Defence case

If the accused is not discharged at the close of the state case, he/she must be brought forward on his/her defence. It is mandatory for the accused himself/herself to be questioned by the prosecutor and the court. This means that even where the accused chooses not to give evidence, he/she is still liable to be questioned. Adverse inferences may be drawn against the accused where he/she refuses to answer questions. Normally, the accused must be the first witness for the defence, although this may be varied by the court in exceptional cases. The defence case is conducted in the same way as the prosecution case: evidence is led through witnesses who give evidence-in-chief and are cross-examined and re-examined.

Close of the defence case

After leading evidence from defence witnesses, the defence team closes its case.

Addresses by both sides

Each side is entitled to address the court summarizing its case and focusing on key issues. If the court refuses to allow the accused to address it, the conviction may be set aside.[27]

Verdict

The verdict is either one of guilty or not guilty. A guilty verdict must only be returned if the court is satisfied beyond reasonable doubt that the accused is guilty.

It is common for charges to be preferred in the alternative. If the evidence proves the accused guilty on both the main charge and all the charges in the alternative, it is not permissible for the court to return a guilty verdict on the main charge and the alternatives as well. Conviction can only be on one charge. The court must choose the most appropriate charge on which to return the verdict of guilty. Conversely, if the evidence proves the accused guilty of only one of the alternative charges, the court must ensure that it returns a verdict of not guilty on those alternative charges not proven.

Addresses on sentence: mitigation/aggravation

If a verdict of guilty is pronounced, the next issue is the passing of an appropriate sentence. Each side is given an opportunity to address the court on the appropriate sentence. If any of the parties wish to lead evidence that is relevant for sentence, this should be done before addresses on sentence commence.

The general rule is that the prosecutor makes his/her address first. The duty of the prosecutor is to assist the court in passing an appropriate sentence, and not necessarily to see to it that the accused is heavily punished. Thus, the prosecutor may draw to the attention of the court any facts favourable to the accused that may mitigate the sentence. In the addresses, note must be taken of 'aggravating' and 'mitigating' factors. Aggravating factors are those that demonstrate the appropriateness of a more severe sentence for the accused while mitigating factors point to a more lenient sentence. The onus of proof of aggravating facts rests on the state. In general, mitigating facts must be established by the accused, but it is permissible for the court to take into account any mitigating facts established by the state case.

Sentencing

The appropriate sentence is determined and pronounced by the court. The law requires that all sentences, except in the few situations where the trial is *in camera*, i.e., closed to the public, be pronounced in an open court. One example of a situation where the trial may be in camera is where the identity of the witness(es) must be protected. The forms of sentence which may be passed are cautions or reprimands; fines; recognisances; community service; imprisonment; corporal punishment; and death. The nature of each of these is outlined below.

Caution or reprimand

Here, the accused is actually discharged but with a caution or reprimand. The effect of this is that in the event of a subsequent conviction, the discharge with a caution or reprimand is treated as a previous conviction for purposes of sentence.

Fines

In *S v Kunesu and Ors*, the following principles captured in the headnote were adopted in relation to the imposition of a fine as a sentence:

> Where an offence warrants the imposition of a fine, the fine imposed must take into account the accused's means, resources and financial responsibilities. The fine must not be set at a level patently beyond the means of the accused person. If an excessive fine is imposed, justice will not be done. Excessive fines lead to people going to prison unnecessarily .... Whilst fines should not be so low as to make serious offences appear trivial, the imposition of fines patently beyond the means of accused persons is an exercise in futility .... This does not always mean that the fine must be within the immediate means of the accused person, though this should normally be so where the offence is not a serious one .... Although fines may be increased somewhat if the accused persons are permitted to pay the fines in instalments, if this option is taken too far it is, in effect, punishing poor persons substantially more severely than rich persons.
>
> Where there is an apparently unbridgeable gap between the accused person's available resources and the appropriate fine for his offence, the court may consider imposing a fine which is suspended on condition the accused carries out appropriate community service.[28]

The Criminal Law Code has provision for a standard scale of fines ranging from level one to fourteen.[29] Most statutes that provide for a fine as the appropriate sentence specify the amount of the fine by reference to a level on the standard scale. However, notwithstanding reference in a statute to a level on the standard scale of fines, whenever a court imposes a sentence of a fine, it must specify the monetary amount of the fine and not its level.[30]

Recognisances

This form of punishment involves the accused being ordered to deposit an amount with the court and keep peace and be on good behaviour for a period fixed by the court. This money will be refunded to the accused if he/she does not breach the conditions imposed within the fixed time period. If he/she breaches the conditions set, the amount deposited will be forfeited to the state.

Community Service

This sentence involves the suspension of imprisonment on condition that the accused performs community service. The service to the community may be of any suitable form, such as working at a community clinic or cleaning the premises of a community school. In *S v Ndhlovu*, Korsah JA stated that:

> Community service is considered as fine on leisure time and is particularly appropriate for persons who exhibit anti-social behaviour. It gives the opportunity for constructive activity as well as a possible change of outlook on the part of the offender. The essentials of an order for community service, all of which must co-exist to render it meaningful, are to punish the culprit, to make him pay reparation by way of his service to the community and to reintegrate him into society.[31]

Imprisonment

This is the most common form of sentence and involves sending the accused person to prison for a specified period. Our courts prefer 'short and effective' periods of imprisonment. Bartlett J emphasized this point in *S v Hwemba*:

> A sentence of imprisonment is a rigorous and severe form of punishment. It should only be imposed as a last resort. Where imprisonment is the only appropriate sentence, a court must impose the minimum effective period to do justice to both the offender and the interests of justice. Overlong imprisonment is counter-productive. It brutalizes and contaminates the offender and

may cause him to redefine himself as a criminal and behave accordingly. This is particularly the case with the first offender who is contrite.

It seems that most magistrates think that 12 to 18 months is by no means a substantial period of imprisonment and that six months is a very short period of imprisonment. But six months for a first offender must seem interminable. Such a period is a substantial punishment and not the short, sharp period that magistrates seem to think it is.[32]

Corporal punishment

The corporal punishment of adults is unconstitutional. This position was emphatically made by the Supreme Court in *S v Ncube*, which found it to be contrary to Section 15 (1) of the Constitution.[33] Gubbay JA (as he then was) stated that:

> The manner in which it is administered ... is somewhat reminiscent of flogging at the whipping post, a barbaric occurrence particularly prevalent a century or so past. It is a punishment, not only inherently brutal and cruel, for its infliction is attended by acute pain and much physical suffering, but one that strips the recipient of all dignity and self-respect. It is relentless in its severity and is contrary to the traditional humanity practiced by almost the whole of the civilized world, being incompatible with evolving standards of decency.
>
> ... No matter the extent of regulatory safeguards, it is a procedure easily subject to abuse in the hands of a sadistic and unscrupulous prison officer who is called upon to administer it. It is degrading to both the punished and the punisher alike. It causes the executioner, and through him society, to stoop to the level of the criminal.[34]

The Supreme Court followed this reasoning in *S v A Juvenile*. It held, by a three-to-two majority, that the corporal punishment of juveniles was also unconstitutional.[35] The government disagreed with this approach and amended the Constitution to make it clear that corporal punishment of *male* juveniles was permissible. Section 15 (3) of the Constitution now provides that:

> No moderate corporal punishment inflicted – (a) in appropriate circumstances upon a person under the age of eighteen years by *his* parent or guardian or by someone *in loco parentis* or in whom are vested any of the powers of his parent or guardian; or (b) in execution of the judgment or order of a court, upon a *male* person under the age of eighteen years as a penalty for breach of any law; shall be held to be in contravention of sub-Section (1) on the ground that it is inhuman or degrading.[36]

Sentencing to death

The death sentence is still available in Zimbabwe, although it has been abolished in many countries, including the United Kingdom and South

Africa. Despite being generally regarded as the world's leading democracy, many of America's 50 states still use the death penalty as the ultimate punishment.

In Zimbabwe, the imposition of the death sentence is limited to two crimes: murder and treason. It is discretionary, not mandatory, for the latter. It is mandatory if a person is convicted of murder unless 'the convicted person is under the age of eighteen years at the time of the commission of the crime or the court is of the opinion that there are extenuating circumstances'.[37] Extenuating circumstances are any circumstances that reduce the accused's moral guilt/blameworthiness. If the court finds that there are no extenuating circumstances, it must undertake a procedure called *allocutus* before passing the death sentence. This procedure entails the registrar of the court asking the accused whether:

> You know of any reason or have anything to say why the sentence of death should not be passed upon you.

If the accused discloses a good reason in the *allocutus*, the court may revisit its finding on extenuating circumstances, otherwise it will proceed to pass the sentence. When the sentence of death is passed by the High Court, it must be confirmed by the Supreme Court and thereafter by the president before it can be executed. The method used in Zimbabwe is hanging.

Notes

1. See p. 64.
2. 1996 (2) *ZLR* 664, 667H-668B.
3. See *Chinamora v Angwa Furnishers (Pvt.) Ltd*, 1996 (2) *ZLR* 664 (5).
4. See Joseph Herbstein and Louis de Villiers van Winsen (1966) *The Civil Practice of the Superior Courts in South Africa*. Second edition. Cape Town: Juta and Co., p. 583.
5. See *Lindsay v Lindsay* (2); *Scheelite King Mining Co (Pvt) Ltd v Mahachi* 1998 (i) *ZLR* 173 (H).
6. See *Lindsay v Lindsay* (2), p. 299B; *Haddow v Haddow* 1974 (i) RLR 5 (G), p. 6A.
7. See *Lindsay v Lindsay* (2).
8. See Mary Welsh (1996) *The Civil Practice Handbook*, Legal Resources Foundation: Harare, p. 10/2.
9. See Section 92 of the Labour Act.
10. See Section 26 of the High Court Act, Chapter 7:06.
11. See Section 76 (4a) of the Constitution of Zimbabwe.

12. Ibid., Section 30.
13. See Privileges and Immunities Act, Chapter 3:03.
14. See *Levy v Benatar* 1987 (1) ZLR 120 (S); *Attorney General v Van de Merwe and Bornman* 1946 OPD 197.
15. See Section 76 (4) (b), *General African Examiner (Pvt) Ltd v Howman & Ors MNO* 1966 RLR 75 (G), 1966 (2) SA 1 (R).
16. 1987(1) ZLR 120(SC).
17. See Section 24 ff of the Criminal Procedure and Evidence Act.
18. Ibid, Section 27 (Chapter 9:07).
19. Ibid., Section 33.
20. Ibid, Section 132.
21. See *Mutambara & Ors v Minister of Home Affairs* 1989 (3) ZLR 96 (H).
22. See Section 180 (6) of the Criminal Procedure & Evidence Act.
23. Ibid. See 194 (1). See also Section 18 (3) of the Constitution of Zimbabwe.
24. See 357 (1); *S v Kamanga* 1991 (2) ZLR 25 (H).
25. See Section 31J of the Constitution of Zimbabwe.
26. See Reid Rowland (1997) *Criminal Procedure in Zimbabwe*. Harare: Legal Resources Foundation, 16-32 and 16-33.
27. Ibid., pp. 16-39.
28. 1993 (2) ZLR 253 (H).
29. See First Schedule of the Criminal Law (Codification and Reform) Act, 2004.
30. See Section 280 (4) of the Criminal Law Code.
31. *S v Ndlovu* S-28-94.
32. 1999 (1) ZLR 234 (H).
33. 1987 (2) ZLR 246 (S).
34. See pp. 273-4.
35. 1989 (2) ZLR 61 (SC).
36. Italics of gender are my emphasis.
37. See Section 47 of the Criminal Law Code.

8

Legal Aid

Introduction

Legal aid refers to the system of providing legal services to persons who are unable to afford to pay fees for such services. This arises in a world in which the cost of legal services is, without exception, very high. Whether or not the state should provide legal aid is a controversial issue. It raises key political questions such as whether or not the state has any obligation towards the poor.

Today, legal aid is almost universally regarded as an aspect of access to justice. In the words of Gail Kuppan:

> Its object is to make it impossible for any person to be denied the equal protection of the law simply on account of poverty. It is an essential part of the administration of justice of any democratic state and is internationally recognized as such.[1]

This approach suggests that there exists a right to the provision of legal aid in the corpus of civil and political rights. It is submitted that this is indeed the case. The right to legal aid is implied in the very notion of the universally accepted and fundamental right of equality before the law. As such, it requires no more justification than that applicable to all human rights: self-evident rights that must be enjoyed by human beings by virtue of being human. The proper administration of justice requires, as a basic minimum, that access to justice be not unduly restricted by the lack of resources to pay legal fees. In other words, the legal system must not condemn poor people to injustice by the mere device of making legal services unaffordable. It is therefore essential for the state to provide some form of legal aid.

The system of legal aid in Zimbabwe is poorly developed. Before the enactment of the Legal Aid Act, 1996, there were two categories of legal aid worth considering, namely, (1) Civil Court legal aid and (2) Criminal Court legal aid.[2] This may be described as the old system of legal aid.

The Old System of Legal Aid

Civil Court Legal Aid

In both the Magistrates Court and High Court there existed a system for the assistance of indigent persons. In the Magistrates Court, the system was known as the *pro deo* system and was governed by the Magistrates Court (Civil) Rules, 1980, Order 5. In terms of Order 5, a person desiring to sue or defend as a 'pauper' could apply to court for legal aid. The court had to be satisfied that (i) the applicant had a *prima facie* right of action or defence and (ii) the applicant had no means sufficient to pay the court fees and messenger's charges. Only then could the court order that a lawyer be appointed to act for the applicant. The requirement that the court be satisfied that the applicant had no means to pay court fees and messenger's charges meant that only the *very poor* qualified for this assistance. Further, the court was not obliged to order the appointment of a lawyer – it could instead simply order that the pleading be served free of charge.

In the High Court, the system was called the *informa pauperis* system. It was governed by the High Court Rules, 1971, Order 44. In terms of Order 44, a person wishing to bring or defend proceedings *in forma pauperis* could apply to the Registrar if he/she was a person whose assets were less than a specified amount, excluding household possessions. If the Registrar was satisfied that the applicant *prima facie* qualified, he/she was required to nominate a legal practitioner to whom to refer the applicant. The legal practitioner had also to satisfy himself/herself that the matter was one in which he/she could act *in forma pauperis*. In other words, the legal practitioner was required to investigate the applicant's means. Once the legal practitioner was satisfied, he/she had to act on behalf of the applicant.

Criminal Court Legal Aid

The Constitution of Zimbabwe does not enshrine a right to legal aid for accused persons. On the contrary, it provides in Section 18 (3) (d) that:

'Every person who is charged with a criminal offence shall be permitted to defend himself in person or, save in proceedings before a local court, at his own expense by a legal representative of his own choice'.

This is reiterated by Section 191 (a) of the Criminal Procedure and Evidence Act; 65 of the Magistrates Court Act and 51 of the High Court Act. However, there was some statutory provision for legal aid in criminal matters. The governing legislation was the Legal Assistance and Representation Act (Chapter 9:13).

The long title of the Act restricted its scope to criminal matters only and was in the following instructive words:

> An Act to provide for the granting of legal assistance to indigent persons appearing in the courts of Zimbabwe in connection with criminal proceedings; to provide for the remuneration of legal practitioners who appear on behalf of such persons and of legal practitioners who appear in the Supreme Court or the High Court at the request of the court.

It provided for two schemes of criminal legal aid: (i) at the instance of the court and (ii) on the initiative of the Attorney General.[3] Legal aid at the instance of the court was stipulated in terms of Section 3 and its provisions were as follows:

> 3. If it appears to a judge of the Supreme Court or the High Court, a registrar or magistrate that –
>   (a) it is desirable, in the interests of justice, that a person who is –
>   (i) standing or about to stand trial before any court; or
>   (ii) appearing or about to appear before a magistrate to undergo a preparatory examination; or
>   (iii) a party in any appeal or application in a criminal matter to the Supreme Court or the High Court
>   should have legal assistance in the preparation and conduct of his defence or in any proceedings incidental thereto or in any proceedings relating to the appeal or application, as the case may be; and
>   (b) the means of that person are insufficient to enable him to obtain the legal assistance referred to in paragraph (a);
>   the judge, registrar or magistrate, as the case may be, may certify, if this has not already been done by any other person authorized to certify under this Act, that that person ought to have such legal assistance.

Section 4 provided for the scheme initiated by the Attorney General. Its provisions were as follows:

> 4. If it appears to the Attorney General that –
>   (a) it is desirable in the interests of justice that a person who –
>   (i) has been indicted for trial before the High Court; or

is appearing or about to appear before a Magistrates Court for the purposes of a preparatory examination or trial; should have legal assistance in the preparation and conduct of his defence or in proceedings incidental thereto, and

(b) the means of that person are insufficient to enable him to obtain the legal assistance referred to in paragraph (a); the Attorney General may certify, if this has not already been done in terms of Section Three, that that person ought to have such legal assistance.

Once a certificate was issued in terms of Section 3 or 4, the person in question became entitled to the services of a legal practitioner provided it was 'practicable to procure the services of a legal practitioner'.[4]

The new system of legal aid

The new system of legal aid is provided for in terms of the Legal Aid Act, 1996.[5] The Act repealed the Legal Assistance and Representation Act (Chapter 9:13) and its long title states that its aim is 'to provide for the granting of legal aid to indigent persons'.

The Legal Aid Act, 1996 establishes a Legal Aid Directorate consisting of a director and law officers.[6] The functions of the Legal Aid Directorate (LAD) are to provide legal aid to eligible persons and to do all things necessary to promote the provision of legal aid.[7] To qualify for appointment as the Director, a person must be a registered legal practitioner.[8] Law officers need not be registered legal practitioners.[9] He/she is subject to policy directions of a general character given by the Minister of Justice.[10] Outside these directions, the Director is not 'subject to the direction or control of any other person or authority'.[11]

To qualify for legal aid, an applicant must satisfy the Director that (i) he/she has insufficient means to obtain the services of a legal practitioner on his own account; (ii) he/she has reasonable grounds for initiating, carrying on, defending or being a party to the proceedings for which he applies for legal aid; and (iii) he/she is in need or would benefit from the legal aid services provided in terms of the Act.[12] In assessing the means of an applicant for purposes of determining whether or not he/she has 'insufficient means', the Director is required to take into account the income and property of the applicant, but must exclude his/her (i) dwelling house; (ii) necessary beds, bedding and clothing; (iii) necessary furniture; (iv) tools and implements for his/her trade or occupation; and (v) food and drink necessary to meet the needs of himself/herself and members of his/her family for one month.[13] The Director is also required to make due allowances for the 'necessary educational needs' of any dependent child of the applicant.[14]

The application for legal aid must be made on the prescribed form. The application form was prescribed by the Legal Aid Regulations, 2002 (Statutory Instrument 303/2002). The form requires the applicant to provide a set of details that includes their marital status, particulars of any dependent children, their occupation and salary (if any), the particulars of any movable property and the nature of the legal problem in issue.

On receipt of an application, the Director is obliged to consider it and either grant or reject it.[15] While an application is always rejected if the applicant is ineligible in terms of Section 8, the mere fact that an applicant is eligible does not automatically lead to the granting of legal aid. Where an applicant is eligible, the Director may only grant legal aid if also satisfied that 'the resources of the Directorate and the Legal Aid Fund will be sufficient to provide the legal aid required'.[16] The Act requires the Director to make his/her decision expeditiously. This is implied from the requirement that he/she communicate his/her decision 'forthwith'.[17] Any person who is aggrieved by a decision of the Director is entitled to appeal to the Minister of Justice.[18]

The Act is nevertheless vague on the nature of legal aid available to successful applicants. Section 11 simply provides as follows:

(1) Legal aid provided in terms of this Act shall include the doing of anything that may properly be done by a legal practitioner for or in the interests of his client.

(2) The nature of legal aid provided to a person in any particular case shall be at the discretion of the Director, taking into account the needs of the person concerned and the resources of the Directorate and the Legal Aid Fund.

In principle, Section 11 (1) makes any form of appropriate legal services available as legal aid. Legal advice and representation in court are clearly covered. However, Section 11 (2) leaves it to the discretion of the Director as to whether or not, in a given case, the legal service provided is legal advice only, legal advice *and* representation in court, or only representation in court. In addition, the amount of time that a legal practitioner may/must spend on a case is also at the discretion of the Director.[19]

Whatever its nature, any legal aid offered may be rendered by a law officer working in the Legal Aid Directorate or by a legal practitioner in private practice.[20] Some law officers are not registered legal practitioners. To enable such law officers to appear in court and to issue summons or other court processes on behalf of a person in receipt of legal aid, the Act temporarily grants them the same rights as legal practitioners.[21] Section 6 states that:

> 6 (1) In any matter in which the provision of legal aid is granted in terms of this Act, a law officer shall:
> (a) have the right of audience in any court;
> (b) have the right to issue out summons or process or commence, carry on or defend any proceedings in any court in the name of an aided person;
> (c) have the right to instruct or assist an aided person to issue out summons or process or to commence, carry on, or defend any proceedings in any court in the same manner and to the same extent as a registered legal practitioner, notwithstanding that the law officer is not so registered.

It appears clear from a reading of the entire Act that its contention is that most legal services required for legal aid should be provided by the law officers. Law officers are employed by the state and are part of the Public Service.[22] It makes the engagement for legal aid, of legal practitioners in private practice, an exception rather than the rule. This is made evident in Section 12, where it makes the engagement of a legal practitioner in private practice conditional on either the Director forming an opinion that 'it is in the interests of justice' to do so or the recommendation of a judge or magistrate or the Attorney General. However, a legal practitioner in private practice who fails or refuses to make himself/herself available for legal aid work may face disciplinary action and have rights of audience before the courts removed or restricted.[23]

The second route to legal aid arises in terms of Section 10 of the Legal Aid Act, where it is at the instigation of a judge or magistrate or Attorney General. This is so in situations where civil or criminal proceedings are in progress or are anticipated and the judge or magistrate or Attorney General forms the view that 'it is desirable in the interests of justice that legal aid should be provided to a person who is or will be a party to the proceedings'.[24] Further, the judge or magistrate or Attorney General must form the view that the person in question 'may have insufficient means to obtain the services of a legal practitioner on his own account'.[25] In such cases, the judge or magistrate or Attorney General makes a recommendation to the Director for the granting of legal aid. Although the Director is not bound by any such recommendation, he/she is obliged 'forthwith' to assess the means of the person concerned according to protocol.

Ultimately, this second route ends at the same gate as the first. The initiative of the judge or magistrate or Attorney General merely replaces the application by the person seeking legal aid. However, it is submitted that the Director must hesitate before rejecting a recommendation made in terms of Section 10 of the Act.

Where legal aid is provided by a legal practitioner in private practice, he/she is entitled to be paid his fees and expenses in agreement with the prescribed tariff.[26] A court before which such a legal practitioner appears may recommend higher fees than those prescribed if the matter is complex or the proceedings are long.[27]

The Act created a Legal Aid Fund for the purposes of funding legal aid.[28] This fund consists of monies appropriated for the purpose by Parliament and other contributions arising from the provisions of Section 15 and 16 of the Act. In terms of Section 15, a person who has been granted legal aid may be required to contribute to the cost to the extent which 'in the opinion of the Director, is just and reasonable having regard to the means of the person concerned'. In terms of Section 16, the Director is empowered to deduct an amount that is prescribed from any damages awarded to an aided person by a court.

Evaluation of the Legal Aid Scheme in terms of the Act

Several points may be made about the legal aid scheme in terms of the Act. First, the Legal Aid Directorate is simply a department in the Ministry of Justice. Its director and the law officers are part of the Public Service and as such the director reports to the Permanent Secretary of the Ministry of justice. Such an arrangement makes the legal aid process neither independent nor impartial, irrespective of the provisions of Section 4 (4), which purport to make the director independent in the discharge of his/her functions. As a general principle, it is essential that the body charged with administering legal aid be independent and impartial. Countries that take the provision of legal aid seriously create independent statutory bodies, for example, the Legal Aid Board of South Africa and the Legal Services Commission of England and Wales.

Secondly, the criteria for eligibility for legal aid is problematic, as Section 8 confers potential eligibility on a person who has 'insufficient means'. The expression 'insufficient means' is not, however, defined.

The guidelines set out in Section 9 as to what the Director must take into account when assessing the means of an applicant do not give sufficient clarity as to who qualifies. Whether or not only the very poor qualify or whether or not some middle-class applicants may successfully obtain legal aid largely depends on the practice of the Legal Aid Directorate.

Thirdly, the availability of legal aid is, in every case, subject to the requirement that 'the resources ... be sufficient to provide the legal aid required'. In the absence of resources by the state, no legal aid can be provided.

Fourthly, not only is access to legal aid tricky but there is also little public information dissemination on this subject. As very few people know about the existence of the legal aid system, the majority are unaware that they can initiate steps towards being granted free legal assistance. Moreover, many cases requiring and deserving legal aid may never reach the courts. Even in those cases that do, very few judicial officers utilize the provisions of Section 10 of the Act. This hugely contrasts with the English legal system, for example, where access to legal aid has been widened by the extensive provision of information as well as the 'duty solicitor scheme', whereby solicitors provide legal assistance at police stations without any formal applications having to be made.

Lastly, Zimbabwe's legal aid scheme does not provide sufficient scope for such services as the provision of legal advice in civil matters or the all-important presence of a lawyer during questioning by the police in criminal matters. It appears that the philosophy of the Legal Aid Act is that legal aid is all about legal representation in court. There is a strong need for the scheme of this Act to be redesigned in order to ensure that adequate scope is provided for essential services other than representation in court. In this respect, the experience of the English legal aid system is worth studying.

Contingency fee arrangements

Since 2000, the legal profession in Zimbabwe has been allowed to enter into contingency fee arrangements. This was introduced by the Legal Practitioners Amendment Act, 2000 (Act No. 10 of 2000), which inserted a new Part IVA into the Legal Practitioners Act. It defines a contingency fee arrangement as 'an agreement entered into between a registered legal practitioner and his client in terms of which no fee, other than court fees or disbursements are payable by the client for the legal practitioner's services in connection with any legal proceedings unless the proceedings result in a decision or settlement in the client's favour'.[29] That one is in place must not be disclosed to the court that hears the legal proceedings concerned.[30]

This is a variant form of legal aid in that poor persons with strong cases may be able to attract a lawyer on the strength of a contingency fee arrangement.

Legal aid by non-governmental organisations

Non-governmental organizations (NGOs) play an important role in the provision of legal aid. In practice, more legal aid flows from these organizations than from the state scheme. The nature of the legal aid provided by each organization depends on its objectives and governing statutes. Some of the more well-known organizations are the Legal Resources Foundation (LRF); the Catholic Commission for Justice and Peace (CCJP); the Zimbabwe Council of Churches (ZCC); the Zimbabwe Lawyers for Human Rights (ZLHR); the Zimbabwe Women Lawyers' Association (ZWLA); the Justice for Children Trust (JCT); the Girl-Child Network (GCN); Musasa Project; and the Zimbabwe Congress of Trade Unions (ZCTU).

A typical service provided by NGOs is that of paralegals. These are non-lawyers who have received basic legal training and provide legal advice in local communities on a wide range of issues. In some cases, they will assist in the drafting of legal documents. The LRF has an extensive programme of paralegals spread across the country. To access their services, one merely has to visit the nearest offices of the LRF. The ZCTU also has paralegals. However, these only provide services to members of its affiliate trade unions. A unique feature of this ZCTU service is that labour legislation permits paralegals, as officials of trade unions, to appear in the Labour Court on behalf of their 'clients'.[31]

Another service offered by NGOs is that of providing qualified legal practitioners to assist the persons concerned. The ZLHR provides legal practitioners to give legal advice and represent persons in court in matters raising an 'issue of human rights'. The JCT says, in its Trust document, that one of its objectives is 'to represent all children in Zimbabwe in all legal issues that pertain to them'. It does this by providing a legal practitioner who represents a child in court on matters that raise issues of children's rights. Similar services are provided by the ZWLA and the GCN.

The law that regulates the operation of NGOs other than trade unions is the Private Voluntary Organisations Act (Chapter 17:05). In terms of this Act, any NGO that seeks to provide funds for legal aid has two options: either it must be registered as a 'private voluntary organization' under the Act or operate as one of the exempted organizations. Among the exempted organizations is 'any trust ... registered with the High Court.'[32] Most NGOs operate as trusts registered with the High Court and therefore do not need registration under the Private Voluntary Organisations Act.

In view of the limited resources of the state, the provision of legal aid by NGOs must be encouraged. This is a point that has not been appreciated by the state authorities in Zimbabwe, who view most NGOs as conduits of opposition politics. For instance, in 2004, Parliament passed the Non-Governmental Organisation Bill, 2004, which sought to repeal the Private Voluntary Organisations Act and introduce a draconian regulatory regime for NGOs. It also sought to ban foreign funding of NGOs and removed trusts from the exemption from registration enjoyed under the current law. However, for some unknown reason, the president did not assent to this bill. Notwithstanding the refusal of the president to assent to the bill, the fact that a government could conceive such a law shows its failure to appreciate the role of NGOs in society.

The English Legal Aid System

Legal aid in England and Wales was introduced immediately after the Second World War. The Labour Government that introduced it saw legal aid as the second of its two pillars of the 'welfare state'. The first pillar was the National Health Service scheme, which was launched in 1948. Legal aid was launched in 1951, having been introduced by the Legal Aid Act, 1949. From inception, its aim was 'to enable people who could not otherwise afford the services of lawyers to be provided with those services by the state.'[33] From 1951 to 1999 (when the current system was introduced), the legal aid system developed through various phases that were driven by legislation. Thus, the Legal Aid Act 1949 gave way to the Legal Advice and Assistance Act 1972, which in turn was replaced by the Legal Aid Act 1988. This latter Act was repealed by the Access to Justice Act 1999 that now regulates the current system of legal aid. However, the current system of legal aid is more or less a continuation of the old system, but with some new elements added by the 1999 Access to Justice Act.

LEGAL AID

The current system of legal aid is managed by a Legal Services Commission (LSC). The LSC was introduced by the 1999 Act and came to replace the Legal Aid Board. It consists of between seven and twelve members who are appointed for their knowledge and experience in matters such as the provision of legal services, the work of the courts, consumer affairs, social conditions and management. Although there appears to be no fundamental difference between the old Legal Aid Board and the new Legal Service Commission, it has been claimed that in moving from the Legal Aid Board to the LSC, 'it was considered necessary to establish a new body to reflect the fundamentally different nature of (the new system of legal aid) .... Membership of the Commission differs from that of the old Legal Aid Board, to reflect a shift in focus from the needs of providers to the needs of users of legal services. Also the Commission is smaller than the Board: seven to 12 members rather than 11 to 17. This is intended to facilitate focused decision-making.'[34]

The LSC's broad mandate is to improve the public's access to legal services and to ensure that the services provided are of good quality. The legal aid system has two schemes, both of which are run by the LSC. These are (i) the Community Legal Service and (ii) the Criminal Defence Service.

The Community Legal Service has taken over, and improved, two aspects of the old legal aid scheme: the 'legal advice and assistance' scheme and civil legal aid. The 'legal advice and assistance' scheme mainly consisted of the provision of legal advice by a solicitor on any questions or issues of English law. This was popularly known as the 'Green Form' scheme. Any solicitor could provide this service to a person who met the eligibility criteria, but the amount of work was subject to a limit of three hours.[35] The solicitor was also responsible for administering the eligibility criteria. Apart from the 'Green Form' scheme, which exclusively related to the giving of legal advice, the 'legal advice and assistance scheme' also had a component called 'assistance by way of representation' (ABWOR). This covered representation in court proceedings where advice had not solved the problems in matters related to proceedings in Magistrates Courts, mental health review tribunals and Family Proceedings Courts. The civil legal aid scheme covered representation for many types of action except libel or slander (defamation).

The main criticisms leveled against the old scheme included (i) that it was administered by solicitors and thus the quality and extent of legal aid depended on what solicitors were prepared to do; (ii) that the limit of up to three hours work was too low; and (iii) that the financial criteria for eligibility were too strict, to the extent that legal aid only became available to a very small number of people.[36]

In order to address some of these criticisms, the Community Legal Service offers a wide range of services. It covers (i) legal help in the form of the provision of legal advice on the application of English law (the old Green Form scheme); (ii) help at court – assistance and advocacy for a client in relation to a particular hearing, but not to the extent of legal representation during proceedings; (iii) approved family help – assistance and representation in family disputes; (iv) legal representation in litigation and advocacy services; (v) support funding, namely, assistance with legal representation in cases which are privately funded; and (vi) family mediation. In addition, the Lord Chancellor is empowered to authorize further services.

Not every solicitor can provide legal aid services. To do so, he/she must have a contract with the Legal Services Commission (LSC). A contract may also be awarded to a 'not-for-profit organization' (known in Zimbabwe as a 'non-governmental organization'). The contract will specify the category of services that may be offered and the amount of work that may be undertaken. After administering the eligibility criteria, a solicitor or a not-for-profit organization holding such a contract can then make decisions as to whether or not to provide legal aid services in a particular case. Aside from 'contract' work, the solicitor or the not-for-profit organization may also perform what is called 'licensed work', which requires the LSC's initial approval of the cost, timing and scope of the legal aid service, on a case by case basis. Once a decision is made to provide legal aid under community legal service, be it of a 'contract' or 'licensed' nature, any of the services listed above may be provided, depending on the circumstances of each case.

The new system was specifically designed to improve the quality of legal aid by creating a framework whereby the LSC may grant contracts only to those who achieve certain minimum standards of quality. It also allows the LSC to monitor the costs of the scheme.

In order to enable greater access to legal aid, the LSC has facilitated the formation of committees in regions and local authority areas. These committees coordinate legal aid within their respective areas. It has also awarded contracts to institutions such as libraries to supply information on legal aid services.

Eligibility for Community Legal Service depends on the applicant meeting the conditions of a means test *and* a merits test. The means test relates to financial eligibility. Standard limits are in place but are reviewed each year. The principle is that persons with very low incomes and little capital must qualify for legal aid. The merits test considers factors such as (i) the potential benefit to the client of providing the service in question; (ii) the cost of providing the service; (iii) the availability and suitability of other sources of funding; (iv) the prospects of success; and (v) the public interest.

The role of the Criminal Defence Service is to secure the provision of advice and representation to people who have been arrested and are being held in custody or who face criminal proceedings (these include criminal trials, appeals and sentencing hearings). As with Community Legal Service, the representative must have a contract with the LSC allowing them to provide legal aid. There are two important components of the Criminal Defence Service, namely the duty solicitor scheme and the public defender service. There are two sides to the duty solicitor scheme: one provides legal advice and assistance to persons who are held in police custody, the other operates at Magistrates Courts. Under the duty solicitor scheme, a solicitor is available 24 hours a day and a person who qualifies for legal aid is entitled to the services of this solicitor. Although the person is still subject to a merits test, most of these services do not require means testing.

Representation in court is not automatic. It is only available where a representation order has been made by the court or the LSC. The public defender service involves delivery of services by lawyers employed by the Criminal Defence Service itself. The services provided are the same as those provided by the duty solicitors, who are lawyers in private practice.

Some of the criticisms levelled against the old duty solicitor schemes included (i) that a duty solicitor was sometimes unavailable when required; (ii) that advice was sometimes provided by a paralegal rather than a solicitor; and (iii) that the quality of the service given was, in some cases, doubtful. The new system has addressed some of these concerns via the contract system under which the LSC will appoint only those solicitors 'competent to undertake Duty Solicitor work'. Further, the duty solicitor scheme also uses a roster, which means that a duty solicitor should always be available.

Apart from state-sanctioned legal aid services, there are a variety of voluntary providers of legal aid. It has been said that there are more than 1,500 not-for-profit advice agencies in England and Wales alone.[37]

In 1995, the English legal system finally accepted the concept of 'contingency fees' as a way of improving access to justice.[38] In a speech delivered in the House of Lords on 23 July 1998, the then Lord Chancellor, Lord Irvine, said:

> These agreements will result in huge expansion of access to justice. Today, only the very rich or the very poor can afford to litigate. In future, everyone with a really strong case will be able to secure his rights free of the fear of ruin if he loses. They will bring the majority of our people into access to justice.[39]

Under this system, a lawyer will only claim fees if he/she wins the case. This means that the litigant will only pay for legal services rendered if he/she is acquitted. It is claimed that in such a system, a person who cannot afford legal fees may have access to a lawyer on the strength of his/her prospects of success. What makes this an aspect of legal aid is that it permits a person who would otherwise be unable to pay legal fees to have access to legal services without having to raise money to meet the costs involved.

Legal Aid in South Africa

Legal aid in South Africa is regulated by two principal pieces of legislation: the Constitution of South Africa[40] and the Legal Aid Board Act.[41] The South African Constitution provides, in relevant provisions of Section 35, as follows:

> 35 ...
>
> (2) Everyone who is detained, including every sentenced prisoner, has the right ...
>
> > (c) to have a legal practitioner assigned to the detained person by the state and at state expense, if substantial injustice would otherwise result, and to be informed of this right promptly ...
>
> (3) Every accused person has a right to a fair trial, which includes the right ...
>
> > (g) to have a legal practitioner assigned to the accused person by the state and at state expense, if substantial injustice would otherwise result, and to be informed of this right promptly.

These provisions mean that the South African Constitution imposes a duty on the state to provide legal aid in criminal cases from the time of the arrest to the trial of an accused person 'if substantial injustice would otherwise result'. There is no constitutional obligation to provide legal aid in civil cases. Outside this specific constitutional aspect of the legal aid, it is the Legal Aid Board Act that governs the system of legal aid in South Africa.

The Legal Aid Board Act established the Legal Aid Board, an autonomous statutory body funded by the state. Its statutory function is to provide legal aid services. Any person seeking legal aid services must make an application to the Legal Aid Board, which has a number of branches countrywide. If there is no local branch available, the local Magistrates Court will represent it. To qualify for legal aid, the applicant must be 'indigent' and have a reasonable prospect of success in the matter in question.

The Act does not, however, define the term 'indigent'. In *Smith v Mutual Federal Insurance Company Ltd*, the court drew a distinction between 'indigent' and 'poor'.[42] It said: 'to be indigent means to be in extreme need or want whereas to be poor means having few things or nothing'.[43] This approach makes an 'indigent' person to be one who is very poor, yet most poor people are above the level of being 'indigent'. To establish whether or not a person is indigent, the Legal Aid Board applies a means test to determine the financial situation of the applicant, taking into consideration such resources as a person's salary, assets and investments. A person who qualifies for legal aid in terms of Section 35 of the Constitution will not be means-tested.

If a person qualifies for legal aid, the Legal Aid Board will appoint him/her a lawyer. There are two legal aid systems that the Board may use, namely, the *judicare system* and the *salaried employee system*. Under the *judicare system*, successful legal aid applicants are referred to lawyers in private practice who then provide the relevant legal services. These lawyers are paid by the Board in terms of a fixed tariff that is laid down by the Board and agreed to by the legal profession.

The *salaried employee system* involves the rendering of legal aid services by salaried employees of the Board. The Board employs qualified lawyers who represent successful legal aid applicants. This is done under what is called the 'Public Defender System'. Apart from the Public Defender System, the salaried employee system also involves Legal Aid Board university law clinics. It is well established that it is cheaper to provide legal aid through the salaried employee system than through the *judicare system*. Recently, the Legal Aid Board expanded its salaried employee system by establishing 'Justice Centres' that also provide legal aid services.

Two main criticisms levelled against the legal aid system administered by the Legal Aid Board are (i) that the definition of 'indigent' is too restrictive – it leaves out many poor people and the middle-class who cannot afford legal fees; and (ii) the bulk of the South African population has no access to the offices of the Legal Aid Board and are thus excluded from legal aid services.

South Africa also has various voluntary providers of legal aid. These include independent university law clinics and non-governmental organizations. Most universities in South Africa operate law clinics that provide practical legal training to law students and free legal services to indigent people. These clinics operate with a Director, candidate attorneys and students. The means test applied at these clinics is less stringent than that of the Legal Aid Board and, in many cases, legal aid is granted to the non-indigent. In addition, non-governmental organizations such as the Lawyers for Human Rights and the Legal Resources Centre provide free legal services. In particular, they litigate in matters of public interest on behalf of persons who cannot afford legal fees charged by private practitioners. They also train paralegals who provide legal services in rural areas.

Notes

1. See G. Kuppan, 'Legal Aid', in M.P. Oliver et al. (2001) *The Extension of Social Security Protection in South Africa – A Legal Inquiry*. Cape Town: Siber Ink, pp. 131.
2. Act No. 18 of 1996.
3. See Sections 3 and 4.
4. See Section 5 of the Act.
5. Act No. 18 of 1996.
6. Legal Aid Act, 1996: Section 3.
7. Ibid., Section 3 (2).
8. Ibid., Section 4 (2).
9. Ibid., Section 6 (1).
10. Ibid., Section 5 (1).
11. Ibid., Section 4 (4).
12. Ibid., Section 8.
13. Ibid., Section 9.
14. See Section 3 (2) of the Legal Aid Regulations, 2002 (Statutory Instruments 303/2002).
15. Legal Aid Act, 1996: Section 7 (2).
16. Ibid., Section 7 (2) (a) (ii).
17. Ibid., Section 7 (2).

18. Ibid., Section 22.
19. Ibid., Section 11 (2).
20. Ibid., Sections 6 and 12, respectively.
21. Ibid., Section 6.
22. Ibid., Section 4.
23. See Section 87 (2) (g) of the Legal Practitioners Act (Chapter 27:07).
24. See Section 10 of the Legal Aid Act.
25. Ibid.
26. Ibid., Section 12 (2).
27. Ibid.
28. Ibid., Section 14.
29. See Section 22 A of the Legal Practitioners Act (Chapter 27:07).
30. Ibid., Section 22 D.
31. See Section 92 of the Labour Act (Chapter 28:01).
32. Ibid., Section 2 of the Act.
33. Slapper and Kelly, p. 575.
34. Ibid., pp. 582-3.
35. Ibid., p. 577.
36. See S.H. Bailey, J. Ching, M.J. Gunn and D. Ormerod (2002) *Smith, Bailey and Gunn on the Modern English Legal System*. Fourth edition. Andover: Sweet and Maxwell, column 10-021.
37. Slapper and Kelly (2004), p. 597.
38. This concept has long been accepted in the United States.
39. Slapper and Kelly (2004), p. 601.
40. Act 108 of 1996.
41. Act 22 of 1969. For a detailed discussion of legal aid in South Africa, see Kuppan in Olivier et al. (2001), pp. 131-63.
42. 1998 (4) SA 626.
43. Ibid., p. 632.

9

Statutory Interpretation

Introduction

The interpretation of statutes falls largely within the realm of the common law. Rules and principles developed by the courts over a long period of time are the mainstay of the interpretation of legislation. However, the Interpretation Act (Chapter 1:01) does provide guidelines for a limited number of legal cases, but it does not direct the courts as to what rule(s) or principle(s) to apply in a given case/situation. Interpretation is thus outside the domain of legislation.

Interpretation is complicated by the very nature of language. Some statutes are incompetently drafted, creating further complications.

The objective of interpretation

The objective of interpretation is to arrive at the *legal* meaning of a statutory provision, i.e., the meaning intended by the legislature. This is not the same as its verbal or grammatical meaning. If that were not so, there would be little purpose in training lawyers. It is generally accepted that the object of statutory interpretation is to arrive at the intention of Parliament or the legislature. To this end, the courts have adopted rules, maxims and presumptions of statutory interpretation and these three (rules, maxims and presumptions) may loosely be described as 'principles' of statutory interpretation. There is, however, no rule or principle that tells the court what rule or principle to apply. Rather, the courts tend to adopt that rule

or principle which is convenient for the case and the decision intended.
In a widely quoted article, John Willis suggests that:

> [A] court invokes whichever of the rules produces a result that satisfies its sense of justice in the case before it. Although the literal rule is the one most frequently referred to in express terms, the courts treat all three as valid and refer to them as occasion demands, but, naturally enough, do not assign any reasons for choosing one rather than another.[1]

F.A.R. Bennion makes the invaluable point that these so-called rules, maxims and presumptions merely constitute 'interpretative criteria' to be weighed, balanced and applied by the courts from case to case. On this, he says:

> The natural and reasonable desire that statutes should be easily understood is doomed to disappointment. Thwarted, it shifts to an equally natural and reasonable desire for efficient tools of interpretation. If statutes must be obscure, let us at least have simple devices to elucidate them. A golden rule would be best, to unlock all mysteries. Alas, as this book demonstrates, there is no golden rule. Nor is there a mischief rule, or a literal rule, or any other cure – all rules of thumb. Instead there are a thousand and one interpretative criteria. Fortunately, not all of these present themselves in any one case; but those that do yield factors that the interpreter must figuratively weigh and balance. That is the nearest we can get to a true golden rule, and it is not very near. If striving could do it, a true golden rule would here be presented to the reader. It can't.[2]

Rules of Statutory Interpretation

There are three rules of statutory interpretation, namely:

1. Literal Rule
2. Golden Rule
3. Mischief Rule

The Literal Rule

Statement of the Rule

If the words of a statute are clear, you must follow them even if they lead to a manifest absurdity.[3]

In construing a statute, the object is to ascertain the intention which the legislature meant to express from the language which it has employed. By far the most important rule to guide the courts in arriving at that intention is to take the language of the instrument as a whole and when words are clear and unambiguous, to place upon them their grammatical construction and give them their ordinary effect.[4]

The essence of the literal rule is to rely exclusively on the language used without paying any regard to the consequences of the interpretation. If the consequences of the interpretation are unfair, unjust, absurd or harsh, it is not the concern of the interpreter.

Application of the Literal Rule

The starting point is to note that the so-called 'ordinary' or 'literal' meaning of a word is not self-evident. What it is to one person maybe different from what it is to another. In the South African case of *Savage v Commissioner for Inland Revenue,* Schreiner JA observed that:

> What seems a clear meaning to one man, may not seem clear to another. The 'literal' meaning is not something revealed to judges by a sort of authentic dictionary: it is only what individual judges think is the literal meaning.[5]

In general, the courts will refer to dictionaries to ascertain the ordinary meaning of a word. Thus, in *Kuvarega v Registrar General,* the court consulted dictionaries to ascertain the meaning of the word 'utter'.[6] The issue before the court involved the interpretation of the phrase 'utter slogans' as used in Section 118 (1) of the Electoral Act. Section 118 (1) provided that, 'no person shall, within 100 metres of any polling station on any polling day utter slogans'. The applicant, who was an opposition candidate in an election, complained that members of the ruling party, ZANU(PF), were in breach of the Act in that they were wearing T-shirts emblazoned with slogans, symbols and pictures of their candidate. It was contended, on behalf of the applicant, that 'utter[ing] slogans' covered the wearing of T-shirts. *The Shorter Oxford English Dictionary* defines 'utter' as 'give vent to (joy, etc.) in sound; to burst out to (a cry, etc.); to give out in an audible voice'. On the basis of the dictionary meaning, the court concluded that the word 'utter' in Section 118(1)(c) denoted the making of a sound. Thus slogans printed on t-shirts were held not covered and therefore not prohibited under the Section.[7]

In *Commercial Farmers Union v Minister of Lands and Others,* one of the issues which arose was whether or not there existed a 'programme of land reform' as contemplated in Section 16A of the Constitution of Zimbabwe.[8] The court referred to the *Oxford English Dictionary* for the meaning of the word 'programme'. The dictionary defined it as 'a definite plan or scheme of any intended proceedings; an outline or abstract of something to be done (whether in writing or not)'.

On the basis of this meaning, it was held that the haphazard occupation of farms by war veterans, villagers and other persons under the so-called 'Fast-Track Plan' was not in accordance with a 'programme of land reform' as provided for in the Constitution.

It must be emphasized that a dictionary meaning is not binding and may be disregarded were the court is of the view that it is not appropriate.[9] Where a word acquires a meaning peculiar to a given community or society, the acquired meaning may be regarded as the 'ordinary' meaning for purposes of the literal rule. For example, South African courts have recognized that in South Africa, the term 'European' refers to every white person, regardless of whether he/she is from Europe, and that 'Asiatic' would never be applied to a white person coming from Asia.[10] Similarly, in Zimbabwe, the expression 'African' would never be used to refer to a white person.

A word that has a technical meaning is not interpreted in its ordinary sense if used in a technical statute. In such a case, it is given its technical meaning. This was succinctly explained by Beadle CJ in *Lonrho Ltd v Salisbury Municipality* in the following words:

> When, in a technical statute like a patent statute, the legislature uses words which for some 300 years have been recognized as having a specialised technical meaning, it must be assumed that the legislature intended to use the words in their recognized technical sense and not in their popular sense, unless, of course it appears from the context in which the words are used that the legislature intended to depart from the proper technical meaning.[11]

The literal rule accepts that words must be interpreted in their context. A word can only be said to be clear and unambiguous after taking into account the context in which it is used. In other words, the ordinary meaning must be qualified by the context. So said Wessels AJA in *Stellenbosch Farmers' Winery Ltd v Distillers Corp (SA) Ltd*:

> It is the duty of the court to read the Section of the Act which requires interpretation sensibly, i.e., with due regard, on the one hand, to the meaning which permitted grammatical usage assigns to the words used in the Section in question, and, on the other hand, to the contextual sense, which involves consideration of the language of the rest of the statute as well as the matter of the statute, its apparent scope and purpose, and within limits, its background.[12]

In the English case of *Attorney General v Prince Ernest Augustus of*

Hanover, Viscount Simonds emphasized the context as follows:

> Words, and particularly general words, cannot be read in isolation; their colour and content are derived from their context. So it is that I conceive it to be my right and duty to examine every word of a statute in its context, and I use context in its widest sense which I have already indicated as including not only other enacting provisions of the same statute, but its preamble, the existing state of the law, other statutes *in pari materia*, and the mischief which I can, by those and other legitimate means, discern the statute was intended to remedy ....

No one should prefer to understand any part of a statute or of any other document before he has read the whole of it. Until he has done so, he is not entitled to say that it, or any part of it, is clear and unambiguous.[13]

Case law is replete with illuminating illustrations of the application of the literal rule. In the *South African case of Ebrahim v Minister of the Interior*, the court considered the expression 'whilst outside the Union'.[14] In terms of the South African Citizenship Act, 1949, it was provided that a South African would lose his nationality if he acquired a foreign nationality 'whilst outside the Union'. The court held that a South African seaman who had applied for British citizenship, falsely claiming to be ordinarily resident in the United Kingdom when in fact he was living in Durban, did not lose his South African citizenship when, at the time he was formerly conferred with British nationality, he was in South Africa. This conclusion came from a literal reading of the expression 'whilst outside the Union' – the seaman was within South Africa when he was granted British nationality. At no point was the court concerned with the broad purpose of the Act of discouraging dual citizenship.

The most recent application of the literal rule occurred in the case of *George Pretorious Pinnel v Minister of Lands, Agriculture and Rural Resettlement and Others*.[15] Here, the court was concerned with the meaning of Section 31E(1) of the Constitution of Zimbabwe which provides, *inter alia*, that:

> The office of a Vice President, Minister or Deputy Minister shall become vacant – (c) upon the assumption of office of a new President.

In the 2002 Presidential election, Robert Mugabe was re-elected and assumed his new term of office on 1 April 2002. However, he did not immediately appoint a new cabinet. Those cabinet ministers who were in office before the re-election simply continued with their pre-existing duties. On 7 May 2002, the Minister of Justice introduced the Land and

Agriculture Amendment Bill, which became law on 10 May 2002. On 29 April 2002, the Minister of Lands and Agriculture signed an acquisition order for the applicant's farm in terms of Section 8 of the Land Acquisition Act. However, as both ministers (and others) only took their oath of office on 26 August 2002, the applicant contended that they had ceased to be ministers in terms of Section 31E (1) as from 1 April 2002, when the president assumed office. Accordingly, both the Land Acquisition Act and the acquisition order were invalid, as they had been introduced or signed by persons who were not ministers at the time. The overriding issue was whether or not President Mugabe was a 'new' president within the contemplation of Section 31E (1) of the Constitution. By a majority of four to one, the Supreme Court followed *Black's Law Dictionary* and held the ordinary and grammatical meaning of the word 'new' to be 'novelty, or the condition of being previously unknown or of recent or fresh origin'. It concluded therefore that a re-elected president cannot be described as 'new'. The result was that the Ministers were validly in office at the relevant times. In a dissenting judgment, Sandura JA held that a new president referred to a newly appointed president, whether or not he/she was an incumbent president who had been re-elected.

In the English case of *Re Rourland*, a doctor and his wife had, before going to the Far East, made identical wills which provided that each left his/her property to the other, but in the event of the other's death 'proceeding or coinciding' with that of the testator, the property was to go to selected alternative relatives.[16] The couple were aboard a small ship that disappeared in the South Pacific and they were never discovered. The question before the court was whether the property of the husband should go to the wife's relatives or to those of the husband. This fell to be decided on the basis of whether or not the wife's death had 'coincided' with that of the husband. The majority (two judges) adopted the literal rule and held that the natural and grammatical meaning of the word 'coincide' is 'simultaneous'. It meant 'coinciding' in point of time and not coincidence in any other respect such as type or cause of death. The property went to the wife's relatives. Lord Denning dissented and took the view that the literal meaning led to an absurdity, as there was no such thing as people dying 'simultaneously'. He interpreted 'coincide' as denoting the same occasion by the same cause. He would have given the property to the husband's relatives.

The Golden Rule

Statement of the Rule

If the words of a statute are clear and unambiguous, they must be applied unless to do so leads to a result which is absurd, and the absurdity is so glaring that it must never have been intended by the legislature.

The ordinary meaning of words must be followed unless this would lead to an absurdity or is at variance with the intention of the legislature.

I believe that ... the Golden Rule is right that we are to take the whole statute together and construe it altogether giving the words their ordinary signification unless when so applied they produce an inconsistency or an absurdity or inconvenience so great as to convince the court that the intention could not have been to use them with their ordinary signification. And to justify the courts in putting in them some other signification which though less proper is one which the court thinks the words will bear.[17]

The essence of the Golden Rule is that the starting point to interpretation is the literal meaning, but this is subject to the consequences. If the consequences lead to a glaring absurdity or to a result so outrageous that the legislature could not have intended it, the literal meaning must be abandoned in favour of some other meaning that the court will arrive at by employing other aids to interpretation.

Application of the Golden Rule

The issue in each case is whether the consequences could be described as leading to a glaring absurdity. What is absurd to one person may not be absurd to another. Two examples will suffice to illustrate the issue of the absurdity that justifies departure from the literal meaning. In *S v Takawira*, the statute made it an offence to be in possession of subversive material. If interpreted literally, the police officer who took possession of the subversive material, the public prosecutor who tendered it as evidence, and the judicial officer who examined it at the trial would all be guilty of the offence.[18] The Literal Rule was abandoned and the word unlawful was read into the statute.[19] In *S v Masiriva* the Golden Rule was applied by Reynolds J, but he found no absurdity to justify a departure from the literal meaning.[20]

The facts were as follows: The appellant was convicted of drunken driving and driving without a licence. Between the time of the commission of the offence and his trial, he obtained a driving licence. The magistrate ordered that this licence be cancelled. The appellant argued that such cancellation was invalid because he did not have a licence at the time of the commission of the offence. In his view, only a licence possessed at the time of the commission of the offence could be cancelled. The relevant provision of the Road Traffic Act read as follows:

> [A] court which convicts a person of an offence ... involving the driving or attempted driving of a motor vehicle shall ... if the person is the holder of a licence, cancel the licence in respect of motor vehicles of the class to which such prohibition from driving extends.

It was argued on behalf of the appellant that the legislature must have intended to cancel a licence held at the time of the commission of the offence. Cancelling a licence that was obtained after the commission of the offence created such a glaring absurdity that it could never have been intended. Reynolds J rejected this contention and held that there was no absurdity:

> At first blush, it does seem to be at least an injustice that an accused person should have his driver's licence cancelled when he only acquired it subsequent to the commission of the offence .... In the instant case, would it not appear to be equally unjust that a licensed driver who commits this offence should suffer a greater penalty than a person in the position of the appellant, when the latter is potentially the greater menace on roads?[21]

The Mischief Rule

The classic formulation of the mischief rule appears in the 1584 English case of Heydons (3 CO REP 7A) as follows:

> [I]t was resolved by them that for the sure and true interpretation of all statutes in general (be they penal or beneficial, restrictive or enlarging of the common law). Herein, four things are to be discerned and considered:
> 1. What was the common law before the making of the Act?
> 2. What was the mischief and defect for which the common law did not provide?
> 3. What remedy the Parliament hath resolved and appointed to cure the disease of the Commonwealth.
> 4. The true reason of the remedy and then the office of the judge is always to make such construction as shall suppress the mischief and advance the remedy. And to suppress subtle invention and evasions for continuance of the mischief and *pro privato comodo*, and add force and life to cure and remedy, according to the true intend of the makers of the Act, *pro bono publico*.

The essence of this rule is to give weight to the purpose of the legislation and is thus described as the 'purposive approach'.

Application of the Mischief Rule

Today, when investigating the purpose of the legislation, the courts now go beyond the statute itself. This was not the case when the mischief rule was formulated.[22]

The special place of a casus omissus

In simple terms, a *casus omissus* is an omission in a statute arising out of error or inadvertence in such a way as to leave out what appears to have been intended by the legislature. The three rules considered above do not in themselves provide a satisfactory approach to a *casus omissus*. Cross describes it as 'the inexplicable and probably inadvertent failure of the draughtsman to use words entirely apt to cover the instant case'.[23] Bennion's view is that it exists when 'the literal meaning of the enactment goes narrower than the object of the legislator'.[24] The question that arises is how the courts should approach a *casus omissus*.

Hiding behind the theory of separation of powers, the courts are extremely reluctant to fill gaps, arguing that this is the prerogative of the legislature. However, in a narrowly defined set of circumstances, albeit in an inconsistent fashion, they have supplied missing words. In *S v Mpofu*, the court held that it would supply the missing words in a statute if there was clear evidence that the omission was a direct result of a printing error.[25] Similarly, Gubbay J (as he then was), commenting on Section 50 (2) of the 1969 Rhodesian Constitution, said that 'it must be construed according to the dictates of common sense and a glaring absurdity avoided, even if to do so necessitates the interpolation of words. I am satisfied that in enacting S50 (2) it must have been in the compilation of the law-maker that the courts of the land would not be bound by a mere draughtsman's or printer's error, which, depending on the nature of the statute and the context in which it appears, could compel a court to make out manifest injustice either to the individual or the state'.[26]

This position was inspired by Beadle CJ in *Van Heerden v Queen's Hotel (Pty) Ltd*, where he said:

> Courts are extremely loath to read into an Act words which are not there. They will only do so when not to do so will lead to an absurdity so glaring that it could never have been contemplated by the legislature.[27]

The approach of the courts appears to be that a *causus omissus* must only be filled in two exceptional cases, namely to (i) correct an obvious drafting or printing error and (ii) avoid a glaring absurdity. This approach has its origins in English law, whose position is summarized by Devenish as follows:

> The contemporary position in English law is that the legislature must be presumed to have exhaustively enacted everything and therefore it is not for the courts to furnish omissions in the language of the statute.[28]

Notwithstanding the reluctance, English law has several examples of courts filling the *casus omissus* to avoid an absurdity. In *Adler v George* the court was faced with Section 3 of the Official Secrets Act 1920 which provided that:

> No person shall *in the vicinity of* any prohibited place obstruct any member of Her Majesty's forces.[29]

The accused was actually on a Norfolk airfield (a prohibited place) when he obstructed a member of the forces. Did the expression 'in the vicinity of' include being 'in' the place in question? The court had no hesitation in convicting the accused. Lord Parker CJ said:

> I am quite satisfied that this is a case where no violence is done to the language by reading the words 'in the vicinity of' as meaning 'in or in the vicinity of'. Here is a Section in an Act of Parliament designed to prevent interference with members of Her Majesty's Forces, among others, who are engaged on guard, sentry, patrol or other similar duty in relation to a prohibited place such as this station. It would be extraordinary, I venture to think it would be absurd if an indictable offence was thereby created when the obstruction took place outside the precincts of the station, albeit in the vicinity, and no offence at all was created if the obstruction occurred on the station itself .... There may of course, be many contexts in which 'vicinity' must be confined to its literal meaning of 'being near in space', but under this Section, I am quite clear that the context demands that the words should be construed in the way I have said.

Maxims of Statutory Interpretation

Maxims of statutory interpretation are sometimes referred to as 'rules of language'. These are not legal rules but are rough guides to the way in which people speak in certain contexts. Cross says this about maxims:

> It is hardly correct to speak of them as rules of language, for they simply refer to the way in which people speak in certain contexts. They are no more than rough guides to the intention of the speaker or writer.[30]

Maxims may be resorted to either in ascertaining the ordinary and grammatical meaning of a provision or in resolving an ambiguity. Seven examples follow below.

'Ejusdem generis'

This literally means 'of the same kind'. Where general words follow a enumeration of things or items of the same class or genus, the general words must be interpreted as restricted only to the things of that particular class. Cockram explains this in the following words:

> Where a list of items which form the genus or class is followed by a general expression, the general expression is, in the absence of a contrary intention in the statute, construed *ejusdem generis* to include only other particular words.[31]

It was also explained by Diplock LJ in *Quazi v Quazi* as follows:

> The presumption then is that the draughtsman's mind was directed only to the genus indicated by the specific words and that he did not, by his addition of the word 'other' to the list, intend to stray beyond its boundaries, but merely to bring within the ambit of the enacting words those species which complete the genus but have been omitted from the preceding list either inadvertently or in the interests of brevity.[32]

For example, in an English statute entitled the 'Sunday Observance Act 1677', it was provided that 'no tradesman, artificer, workman, labourer or other person whatsoever, shall do or exercise any worldly labour, business, or work of their ordinary callings upon the Lord's Day'. It was held that the expression 'other person whatsoever' must be restricted to 'other persons' following callings of the similar kind to those specified. A barber was held not covered.[33]

In the South African case of *Sacks v City Council of Johannesburg*, the court considered a traffic by-law which provided that 'no person shall sit or lie down on any street, nor shall any person stand, congregate, loiter or walk, or otherwise act in such manner as to obstruct free traffic'.[34] It was held that the general words 'otherwise act in such manner as to obstruct traffic' must be restricted to the same character, as the particular words referred to an obstruction by a direct physical act of the accused. The obstruction was caused by a crowd that had gathered to listen to the accused, who was speaking during an industrial dispute from a car in a public street. The accused himself had not obstructed anything.

For the maxim to apply, the items enumerated must constitute a genus.[35] A genus is a reasonably identifiable category of items or values and must have at least two members.[36] In *S v Makandigona*, the Prevention of

Corruption Act referred to 'any receipt, account or other document'.[37] The court took the view that no genus was created by 'receipt' or 'account' and dismissed the contention that the 'genus' was one of 'documents relating to money'. While it accepted that an 'account' is associated with money, it noted that a 'receipt' could be an acknowledgement of something else other than money. In the absence of a genus, the court declined to apply the *ejusdem generis* rule and gave the expression 'other documents' its ordinary grammatical meaning. Accordingly, it held that the rule applied to the issuing of a certificate of competence by a driving examiner to a woman indicating that she had passed when in fact she had not. Similarly, in *Amberley Estates (Pvt) Ltd v Controller of Customs and Excise* the court had to consider the scope of the definition of 'manufacture' in Section 2 of the Customs and Excise Act.[38] This section provided that 'manufacture' includes 'the mixing, brewing, distilling or production of goods'. It was argued that on the basis of the *ejusdem generis* rule that the word 'mixing' had to be qualified by these same words. The court rejected this argument on the following basis:

> For this rule to operate, there must be a distinct genus or category to which the wide general word is to be linked .... And I cannot accept that the words following upon 'mixing', particularly, 'or production of goods', constitute a definite or clear class.[39]

A genus need not be of an obvious kind and the courts may find a genus from any reasonably identifiable category of items. An example is the English case of *R v Staniforth*.[40] A Section of the Obscene Publications Act, 1959, provided a defence to proceedings relating to the possession for gain of obscene articles on the basis that 'it is proved that publication of the article in question is justified as being for the public good on the ground that it is in the interests of science, literature, art or learning, or other objects of general concern'. It was held that 'other objects of general concern' was limited to these 'interests' alone and so did not cover the 'psychotherapeutic benefit of the pornographic material', i.e., their effect on sexual behaviour and attitudes.

The *ejusdem generis* rule does not apply if it defeats a clear purpose of the legislation or is contrary to the clear intentions of the legislature. In such cases, the words are given their wider meaning in order to accord with the legislative object. For example, it is inappropriate to resort to the rule where the statute uses the word 'include'.[41] Thus, in *S v Van der Merwe*, the statute defined 'fuel' as 'includes diesel oil, gas, petrol or any other substance capable of being used as a fuel'.[42] Although the accused was charged with using methanol (a combustible liquid), the magistrate applied the *ejusdem generis* rule and limited this definition to oil-based products. As methanol is not an oil-based product, he acquitted the accused. On appeal by the Attorney General, this was reversed – the Appeal Court held that the expression 'any substance' clearly referred to any other fuel that could be used to operate a car engine.

'Noscitur a sociis'

This maxim literally means, 'a thing is known by its associates'. It is a broader linguistic rule that refers to the fact that words derive their meaning from the words which surround them. (In fact, the *ejusdem generis* rule is an application of this wider rule). In *Bourne v Norwich Crematorium Ltd*, Stamp J said:

> English words derive colour from those which surround them. Sentences are not mere collections of words to be taken out of the sentence, defined separately by reference to the dictionary or decided cases, and then put back into the sentence with the meaning which you have assigned to them as separate words.[43]

For example, in *Abrahams v Cavey*, the accused was charged with contravening Section 2 of the Ecclesiastical Courts Jurisdiction Act 1860 which penalised 'riotous, violent, or indecent behaviour' in churches and churchyards.[44] The accused had shouted out during a Methodist Church Service (held in connection with the Labour Party Conference), 'Oh you hypocrites, how can you use the word of God to justify your policies?' It was held that the word 'indecent' did not have its usual sexual connotation, but, because of the surrounding words, it must be taken to refer to the indecency, i.e., impropriety, of causing a disturbance within a sacred place.

'The rule of rank'

This is a particular application of the maxim *'noscitur a sociis'*. It is applied where a string of items of a certain level is followed by general words. In that case, it is presumed that the general words are not intended to include items of a higher rank. The favourite illustration is the statement by Blackstone in the following words:

> A statute, which treats things or persons of an inferior rank, cannot by any general words be extended to those of a superior. So a statute, treating of deans, prebendaries, parsons, vicars and others having spiritual promotion, is held not to extend to bishops, though they have spiritual promotion, deans

being the highest persons named, and bishops being of a still higher order.[45]

In *Gregory v Fearn* it was held that the string 'tradesman, artificer, workman, labourer or other person whatsoever' did not include persons above the artisan class.[46] In *Casher v Holmes* the string 'copper, brass and tin, and all other metals' was not taken to include precious metals such as gold and silver.[47]

'Expressio unius est exclusio alterius'

Here, the literal meaning is that the express mention of one or more things is to exclude the others of the same class that are not mentioned. Bennion aptly explained the application of this maxim as follows:

> [I]t is applied where a statutory proposition might have covered a number of matters but in fact mentions only some of them. Unless these are mentioned merely as examples, or *ex abundanti cautela*, or for some other sufficient reason, the rest are taken to be excluded from the proposition.[48]

A leading example is the English case of *Lead Smelting Co v Richardson*.[49] The Poor Relief Act, 1601, imposed a poor rate on the occupiers of 'lands, houses, tithes, and coal mines'. The court held that the express mention of 'coal mines' meant that the word 'lands' did not include mines. Thus, the argument that mines other than coal mines were included under 'lands' was rejected. In *Intro Properties (UK) Ltd v Sauvel*, the Diplomatic Privileges Act 1964 protected, in relation to a foreign mission (diplomatic offices/residences), what were defined as the physical 'premises of the mission'.[50] The definition of this phrase in the legislation was:

> [T]he buildings or parts of buildings and the land ancillary thereto, irrespective of ownership, used for the purposes of the mission including the residence of the head of the mission.

The court had to determine whether or not the private dwelling occupied by a financial counsellor at the French Embassy in London was protected. It was held that the specific mention of the residence of the Head of Mission excluded the residences of the other members of the mission.

This maxim does not apply where its application would lead to a defeat of the legislative intention. In this regard, it is important to bear in mind what Cross has said, namely:

> It is doubtful whether the maxim does any more than draw attention to a fairly obvious linguistic point, viz., that in many contexts the mention of some matters warrants an inference that other cognate matters were intentionally excluded. Allowance must always be made for the fact that the *'exclusio'* may

have been accidental, still more for the fact that there may have been good reason for it.[51]

It was on this basis that the Rhodesian Appellate Division refused to apply the *expressio unius* rule in *R v Barrington*.[52] The statute had specifically penalized persons who unlawfully 'offer to sell gold' and was silent on those who 'offer to buy gold'. It was held that to apply the maxim to exclude the latter would defeat the intention of the legislature.

'Contemporanea expositio'

This arises from the maxim *'contemporanea expositio est optima et fortissima in lege'* (contemporaneous exposition is the best and most powerful in law). A 'contemporaneous exposition' is the meaning of a provision as understood at the time it was originally enacted or shortly thereafter. Cross distinguishes between two forms of contemporary exposition as follows:

> Contemporary exposition may refer, firstly, to the way a text was interpreted by courts, legal writers and others in the period following its enactment. This shows how the statute was understood by those to whom it was addressed. Contemporary exposition may refer, secondly, to statements or statutory instruments issued by the government contemporaneously with the Act. This shows how the Act was understood by those responsible for its enactment.[53]

A contemporary exposition is relevant either where the words are unclear or in pursuit of the legislative purpose. *Contemporanea expositio* is different from *subsecuta observatio* (the usage of a word over a long period of time). Under this latter approach, courts rarely disturb an interpretation that has long and publicly been acted upon.[54] In the English case of *Hanlon v Law Society*, the House of Lords suggested some guidelines on how contemporary exposition through statutory instruments may be utilized. Lord Lowry said:

> Regulations made under [an] Act provide a Parliamentary or administrative contemporary exposition of [this] Act but do not decide or control its meaning: to allow this would be to substitute the rule-making authority for the judge as interpreter and would disregard the possibility that the regulation relied on was misconceived or *ultra vires* ... where the Act provides a framework built on by contemporaneously prepared regulations, the latter may be a reliable guide to the meaning of the former.[55]

'Reddendo singula singulis'

This maxim literally means 'arranging or applying each to each'. Its application is expressed as follows in Bennion:

STATUTORY INTERPRETATION

Where a complex sentence has more than one subject, and more than one object, it may be the right construction to *render each to each*, by reading the provision distributively and applying each object to its appropriate subject. A similar principle applies to verbs and their subjects, and to other parts of speech.[56]

Two examples that illustrate this maxim are:

1. 'Men and women may become members of fraternities and societies'. This can be interpreted as being gender-specific, i.e., that men may become members of fraternities and women members of societies.[57]
2. 'Anyone who shall draw or load a sword or gun' can, however, be interpreted as *anyone* who draws a sword or load a gun.[58]

In the English case of *Overseers of Wigton v Overseers of Snaith*, the issue concerned interpretation of Section 5 of the Poor Law Amendment Act 1849.[59] This provided for the transfer of a lunatic pauper from one poor law union to another and gave the receiving union a right to compensation from the other. This right was expressed as one to receive the expenses incurred 'in and about the obtaining any order of justices for the removal and maintenance of a lunatic pauper'. The question that arose was whether or not the receiving union could claim for the ongoing maintenance of the pauper. The wording, on the face of it, suggested that what could be claimed was not the maintenance per se, but only costs of obtaining an order from the justice for the removal and maintenance. It turned out that an order of the justices was required only for removal and not for maintenance. The court held that the intention was to give a right to compensation for two separate issues, namely (a) the cost of obtaining the removal order, and (b) the ongoing maintenance of the pauper. This interpretation was arrived at by assigning the phrase 'in and about' to each of the removal order and the maintenance of the pauper. The Section was subsequently rephrased to read: 'The receiving union shall be entitled to the expenses incurred 'in and about' the obtaining any order of justices for the removal of a lunatic pauper and 'in and about' the maintenance of a lunatic pauper so removed.'

'Cessante ratione legis, cessat ipsa lex'

The meaning of this maxim is 'if the reason for the law falls away, the law falls away'. A widely quoted example is Willes CJ in *Davis v Powell*:

Reason is the soul of the law, and when the reason of any particular law ceases, so does the law itself.[60]

Taken literally, this maxim has little application in modern statutory interpretation because the courts can neither modify nor repeal a statute on the basis of changed circumstances. However, it may be employed to give effect to the intention of the legislature in circumstances that justify making some provisions of a statute inoperative.

The maxim was applied by Gubbay J (as he then was) in *S v Mujee*.[61] The accused had been convicted by the Magistrates Court of failing to make payments under a contribution order made in terms of the Maintenance Act (then Chapter 35). The contribution order had been made by a juvenile court in respect of his minor child who had been placed under a certified institution. The payments were ordered to be made to the named institution. The accused had been convicted of failing to make payments for the period 1 April 1980 to 1 August 1980. However, it emerged that the minor child had, in fact, been discharged from the named certified institution on 28 February 1980, but that the order requiring the accused to make payments had not been withdrawn. The High Court set aside the accused's conviction by applying the maxim '*cessante ratione legis cessat ipsa lex*'. Gubbay J (as he then was) had this to say:

> It seems to me that, if ever there was a case in which this maxim applies, it is the present. The *ratio* for the contribution order was to compel the accused in the fulfilment of his parental duty of support – to contribute towards the cost incurred by the certified institution in maintaining his child. The *ratio* fell away completely with the removal of the child from the certified institution in February 1980. It could not have been the intention of the lawmaker to treat as valid a maintenance or contribution order when the entire object for which the order was made has ceased to exist.[62]

Presumptions of Statutory Interpretation

Introduction: What are presumptions?

Presumptions of statutory interpretation may be described as assumptions that the courts take into account in interpreting statutory provisions. In the absence of a clear indication to the contrary, a statutory provision is taken to have the meaning arrived at by employing the assumptions. Cross aptly classifies presumptions under two groups: *presumptions of general application* and *presumptions for use in doubtful cases*.[63] Presumptions of general application are fundamental legal principles that should always be kept in mind, even where the language is clear and unambiguous. They are presumed to apply unless excluded by express words or necessary implication. It has been said of such presumptions that:

STATUTORY INTERPRETATION

To begin with, many of the relevant presumptions are legal principles, comprising a basic or fundamental part of the legal system. Statutes ... are not isolated phenomena but should be integrated or harmonized with the whole legal system of which they form a part. It follows, therefore, that such presumptions should be taken into account by the interpreter, right from the outset, no matter how wide and general, and no matter how seemingly clear, the words of the enactment may seem considered in isolation. Furthermore, when all the relevant contextual considerations have been duly weighed, the interpreter should again test his conclusions in the light of the presumptions.[64]

Examples of presumptions that fall in this category are (i) the presumption that *mens rea* (legal intention) is required in statutory crimes; (ii) the presumption that statutory powers must be exercised reasonably; (iii) the presumption that administrative tribunals and other such bodies will act in accordance with the principles of natural justice; and (iv) the principle that no person shall be allowed to gain an advantage from his/her own wrong. An illustration of the fact that this group of presumptions apply – even where the language is clear and unambiguous – is *R v Chief National Insurance Commissioner, ex p Connor*, where the Court was faced with Section 24(1) of the Social Security Act 1975. It provided that:

> A woman who has been widowed shall be entitled to a widow's allowance.[65]

Notwithstanding this clear language, the court applied the principle that no person shall be allowed to benefit from his/her own wrong, and held that a woman who killed her husband and was subsequently convicted of manslaughter (culpable homicide) was not entitled to a widow's allowance under Section 24 (1). In *R v Secretary of State for the Home Department ex p. Puttick* the court disregarded the very clear and absolute terms of Section 6 (2) of the British Nationality Act 1948 and held that Astrid Proll, who had achieved a marriage with a British citizen by the crimes of fraud, forgery and perjury was not entitled to registration as a British citizen.[66]

Presumptions for use in doubtful cases apply where the language of a provision is equivocal. Most presumptions fall in this group. Courts have described them as announcements to the legislature that certain meanings will not be assumed unless expressed in clear terms. In the absence of clear terms, the courts will follow the presumption. Examples of presumptions that fall in this category are (i) presumption against changes in the common law; (ii) presumption against ousting the jurisdiction of the courts; (iii) presumption in favour of individual liberty; and (iv) presumption against retrospective legislation.

Specific Presumptions

The presumption against the alteration of the Common Law more than is necessary

Here, the presumption is to the effect that, in the absence of clear language, either by express words or necessary implication, the courts will not rule that the legislature intended a significant departure from the common law. In other words, it requires statutes to be construed, as far as possible, in conformity with the common law, rather than against it. The presumption requires clear and unequivocal language to alter the common law. In principle, therefore, if the wording evinces a clear intention to alter the common law, then full effect must be given to that intention. In Zimbabwean law, this presumption was defended by Beadle CJ in *Van Heerden & Others No v Queens Hotel (Pty)* in the following terms:

> I cannot see how statutory rights can be regarded as more sacrosanct than a 'common law' right ... as the rights of man are founded on the 'common law' and as the 'common law' is less subject to change than statutory law, which may vary from year to year according to the whim of a particular legislature, common law rights must be more jealously guarded than statutory ones.[67]

In English law, the leading case on the presumption is *Black-Clawson International Ltd v Papierwerke Waldhof – Aschaffenburg Attorney General*, where Lord Reid said:

> This is a presumption which can be stated in various ways. One is that in the absence of any clear indications to the contrary, Parliament can be presumed not to have altered the common law further than was necessary to remedy the 'mischief'. Of course, it may and quite often does go further. But the principle is that if the enactment is ambiguous, that meaning which relates the scope of the Act to the mischief should be taken rather than a different or wider meaning which the contemporary situation did not call for.[68]

One leading example of the *application* of the presumption is the English case of *Leach v R*.[69] Here, Section 4 (1) of the Criminal Evidence Act 1898 provided that the spouse of a person charged with an offence under any statute 'may' be called as a witness either for the prosecution or for the defence. Under the common law, a wife could not be compelled to give evidence against her husband. The House of Lords relied on the presumption and held that Section 4 (1) did not alter the common law: it only made the wife a competent witness for the prosecution but she remained not compellable. The court emphasized the presumption as follows:

> The principle that a wife is not to be compelled to give evidence against her husband is deep seated in the common law of this country, and I think if it is to be overturned it must be overturned by a clear, definite and positive enactment, not by an ambiguous one such as the Section relied upon in this case.

The presumption was applied by the Zimbabwean Supreme Court in *Hama v NRZ*.[70] The Supreme Court was called upon to interpret SI 371/85 on the termination of employment. A previous decision by the Court had held that where it was proven that an employee was not guilty of the misconduct that formed the basis of his/her suspension from employment, the employer would be compelled to reinstate the employee. The employer had no option to pay damages in lieu of reinstatement. In this case, the Supreme Court was reminded of the presumption against alteration of the common law, and was asked to review its previous decision.

The Supreme Court subsequently reversed its previous decision, holding that the principle that an employer cannot be forced to keep an employee it no longer wants was deep seated in the common law and the language of the statutory instrument was not sufficiently clear to oust this common law position.

The presumption that the legislature does not intend that which is harsh, unjust or unreasonable

The cornerstone of this presumption is the natural law thesis that law should be just. Bennion asserts that 'it is a principle of legal policy that law should be just, and that court decisions should further the ends of justice'.[71] The presumption was stated in the following terms by Wessels JA in *Principal Immigration Officer v Bhula*:

> It has been repeatedly laid down by the court that where a statute is clear, the court must give effect to the intention of the legislature however harsh its operations may be to individuals affected thereby. Where, however, two meanings may be given to a Section, and the one meaning leads to harshness and injustice, whilst the other does not, the court will hold that the legislature rather intended the milder than the harsher meaning.[72]

In view of the doctrine of separation of powers, the presumption is clearly rebuttable. Thus, where a statute is unequivocal in its import, the court must give effect to the meaning, no matter how unjust it may be. In the South African case of *R v Sachs*, Centlivres CJ stated:

> [C]ourts of law do scrutinize such statutes with the greatest care but where the statute under consideration in clear terms confers on the executive autocratic powers over individuals, courts of law have no option but to give effect to the

will of the Legislature as expressed in the statute.[73]

This presumption is the basis of the following rules:
1. The legislature is presumed not to have intended to deprive an individual of existing vested rights.
2. Taxation statutes should be strictly construed.
3. Penal Statutes should be strictly construed.

The following cases offer examples of how these rules have been applied.

In *Dadoo Ltd & Others v Krugersdorp Municipality* 1920 AD 530 at 552, Innes CJ said:

> [I]t is a wholesome rule of our law which requires a strict construction to be placed upon statutory provisions which interfere with elementary rights. And it should be applied not only in interpreting a doubtful phrase, but in ascertaining the intent of the law as a whole.

Although this is of doubtful correctness, De Villiers JA stated emphatically that:

> As I understand the principle of all fiscal legislation, it is this: if the person sought to be taxed comes within the letter of the law, he must be taxed, however great the hardship may appear to the judicial mind to be. On the other hand, if the crown, seeking to recover the tax, cannot bring the subject within the letter of the law, the subject is free, however apparently within the law the case might otherwise appear to be. In other words, if there be an equitable construction, certainly such a construction is not admissible in a taxing statute.[74]

In the English case of *W.T. Ramsay Ltd v Inland Revenue Commissioner*, Lord Wilberforce said:

> A subject is only to be taxed upon clear words, not upon 'intendment' or upon the 'equity' of an Act. Any taxing Act of Parliament is to be construed in accordance with this principle. What are 'clear words' is to be ascertained upon normal principles: these do not confine the courts to literal interpretation.[75]

In the English case of *Truck & Sons v Priester*, Lord Ester said:

> [I]f there is a reasonable interpretation which will avoid the penalty in any particular case, we must adopt the construction. If there are two reasonable constructions we must give the more lenient one. That is the settled rule for construction of Penal Sections.[76]

The presumption of constitutionality

This presumption arises in almost every constitutional democracy where the Constitution is the supreme law of the land. In essence, the presumption

STATUTORY INTERPRETATION

operates this way: an Act of Parliament is presumed to be constitutional until the contrary is shown. Further, if a provision is capable of more than one meaning, with one of the possible interpretations falling within the meaning of the Constitution while others do not, it will be presumed that the legislature intended to act constitutionally and that one possible meaning within the Constitution will be adopted. The leading case in Zimbabwe is *Zimbabwe Township Developers (Pvt) Ltd v Louis Shoes (Pvt) Ltd*.[77] Here, the Supreme Court identified two senses in which the presumption of constitutionality can be understood. Georges CJ said:

> Arguments have also been addressed at some length on the presumption of constitutionality. It is a phrase which appears to me to be pregnant with the possibilities of misunderstanding. Clearly, a litigant who asserts that an Act of Parliament or a Regulation is unconstitutional must show that it is. In such a case, the judicial body charged with deciding that issue must interpret the Constitution and determine its meaning and thereafter interpret the challenged piece of legislation to arrive at the conclusion as to whether it falls within that meaning or it does not. The challenged piece of legislation may, however, be capable of more than one meaning. If that is the position then if one possible interpretation falls within the meaning of the Constitution and others do not, then the judicial body will presume that the law-makers intended to act constitutionally and uphold the piece of legislation so interpreted. This is one of the senses in which a presumption of constitutionality can be said to arise. One does not interpret the Constitution in a restricted manner in order to accommodate the challenged legislation. Thereafter the challenged legislation is examined to discover whether it can be interpreted to fit into the framework of the Constitution ....
>
> Because the person alleging unconstitutionality must establish it, a burden may rest on that person to establish factually that an act does not fall within the ambit of constitutionality.[78]

From these remarks, the two senses in which the presumption may be understood are: (i) where a provision is capable of more than one meaning one of which is within the Constitution, it is presumed that the legislature intended that meaning which is within the Constitution; and (ii) where it is sought to be established whether or not a provision is reasonably justifiable in a democratic society, it is presumed that the provision is reasonably justifiable and the onus lies on the challenger to prove the contrary. The justification for the presumption in the second sense was given as follows:

> In that sense, the presumption represents no more than the Court adopting the view that a legislature, elected by universal adult suffrage and liable to be defeated in an election, must be presumed to be a good judge of what is reasonably justifiable in a democratic society.[79]

The presumption of constitutionality has been discussed in other cases: *CW v Commissioner of Taxes*[80] and *Associated Newspapers of Zimbabwe (Private) Limited v (1) The Minister of State for Information and Publicity.*[81]

The presumption against retrospectivity

In terms of this presumption, unless the contrary intention is clear, a statute is not presumed to have an intentional retrospective operation. In *Mahomed No v Union Government*, Innes CJ said:

> The principle that, in the absence of expressed provision to the contrary, no statute is presumed to operate retrospectively is one recognized by the civil law as well as by the law of England. The law-giver is presumed to legislate only for the future.[82]

In *Principal Immigration Officer v Purshotam*, Stratford JA noted that:

> The rule of interpretation is well established, it is that where in express terms or by necessary implication (which is much the same thing) the enactment is to have retrospective effect, that effect must be given to it whatever the consequences may be. If, on the other hand, the clear intention to have a retrospective effect cannot be extracted from the words used in their context, then the enactment must not be taken to affect pre-existing rights.[83]

In the case of *Bater & Anor v Muchengeti*, Gubbay CJ expressed the presumption as follows:

> The correctness of that view of the matter is underscored when account is taken to the fundamental rule of construction in our law, dating probably from Codex 1:14:7, that there is not to be given to an enactment so as to remove or in any way impair existing rights or obligations, unless such a construction appears clearly from the language used or arises by necessary implication. The supposition is that the law-maker intends to deal only with future events and circumstances.[84]

The presumption has arisen in a number of cases. Key examples include *Agere v Nyambuya* (1985) (2) ZLR 336 (S),[85] and *Nkomo & Anor v A-G* (1993) (2) ZLR 422 (S).[86]

The presumption in favour of the principles of natural justice

Devenish presents this presumption as follows:

> It has been clearly established in our law that when a statute authorizes judicial or quasi-judicial powers which may influence individual or property rights, there is a presumption that, in the absence of an express provision or a clear

intention to the contrary, the powers so given are to be exercised in accordance with the principles of natural justice.[87]

There are two main principles of natural justice, namely (i) *audi alteram partem* rule (a person must be given the right to be heard before an adverse decision is taken) and (ii) the *nemo judex* principle (a person must not be judge in his/her own cause). The *audi alteram partem* rule is the most significant of the two and has arisen in a number of cases.

For example, in *Health Professionals Council v McGowan,* the Practice Control Committee of the Health Professionals Council, acting in terms of Section 39D(2) of the Medical, Dental and Allied Professions Act, imposed certain restrictive medical practice conditions upon McGowan (the medical practitioner).[88] The Committee did not afford the medical practitioner an opportunity to make representations before the decision was made to impose the restrictive conditions. Section 39(D)(2) did not expressly provide for a right to make representations by the medical practitioner. The presumption in favour of the principles of natural justice was invoked and it was held that the medical practitioner should have been given an opportunity to be heard before the decision was made.

In *Zimbabwe Teachers Association & Ors v Minister of Education*, the government summarily dismissed all striking teachers who had not heeded its call for their return to work by a set date.[89] The dismissals were in terms of Section 5(1)(c) of the Emergency Powers (Maintenance of Essential Services) Regulations, 1989, which provided that:

> if an employee without lawful excuse:
>> declares or takes part in or advises, encourages, incites, commands, aids or procures another person to declare or take part in a strike or the continuation of a strike; his general manager or a designated officer may –
>>> (i) suspend the employee from duty for a period not exceeding three months, or
>>> (ii) summarily dismiss the employee from his employment.

The teachers challenged their dismissal on, *inter alia*, the basis that the summary dismissal was unlawful for failure to comply with the *audi alteram partem* rule. The court had to consider whether or not the wording of the regulations ousted the application of the principle. In the absence of clear words to that effect, the court held that the rule had not been excluded and declared the dismissals unlawful for their failure to comply with the *audi alteram partem* rule.

Ebrahim JA had this to say on the matter:

An employee is afforded an opportunity to show he has a lawful excuse for not performing his duties although the onus rests on him to establish this. I can find no words in the rest of the provisions of the Regulations which indicate expressly or by implication, a clear intention that the individual's right to be heard is excluded ... I am satisfied that the opening words of S5(1) of the Regulations are designed to give the teachers an opportunity to make representations.[90]

The presumption against interpreting a statute so as to oust or restrict the jurisdiction of the Superior Courts

In relation to this presumption, in *De Wet v Deetlefs* Solomon CJ stated:

It is a well-recognised rule in the interpretation of statutes that, in order to oust the jurisdiction of a court of law, it must be clear that such was the intention of the legislature.[91]

This presumption has little relevance in a constitutional democracy with a justiciable Bill of Rights. In Zimbabwe, Section 18 entitles every person to the protection of the law while Section 79 provides for an independent judiciary. Thus, an Act of Parliament that purports to oust the jurisdiction of the superior courts may be declared unconstitutional.

The presumption that a statute will not be interpreted so as to violate a rule of international law or international obligations

This presumption requires the courts to seek an interpretation of a statute that will not make domestic law conflict with international law.[92]

Aids to Statutory Interpretation

The Interpretation Act (Chapter 1:01).

The Interpretation Act (Chapter 1:01) applies to all enactments in Zimbabwe. Section 2 provides as follows:

(i) The provisions of this Act shall extend and apply to every enactment – except in so far as any such provisions:
   (a) are inconsistent with the intention or object of such enactment; or
   (b) would give to any word, expression or provision of any such enactment an interpretation inconsistent with the context; or
   (c) are in such enactment declared not applicable thereto.

(ii) Nothing in this Act shall exclude the application to any enactment of any rule of construction applicable thereto and not inconsistent with this Act.

It is clear from Section 2 that while the Interpretation Act applies to every enactment, it does not affect the application of rules, maxims and presumptions of statutory interpretation and may be ousted by either the context or provisions of the enactment being considered.[93]

The Interpretation Act contains some standard definitions to be applied to every enactment in the absence of contrary provisions. It also contains some substantive rules of law. It has been suggested that the objects of an Interpretation Act are '(1) to shorten and simplify written laws by the avoidance of needless repetition; (2) to promote consistency of form and language in written laws; and (3) to clarify the effect of laws by the enactment of rules of construction'.[94]

The Act begins with a set of definitions that must apply 'in every enactment' unless the contrary is indicated. Examples include:

- 'African' means '(a) any member of the aboriginal tribes or races of Africa and the islands adjacent thereto, including Madagascar and Zanzibar or (b) any person who has the blood of such tribes or races and who lives as a member of an aboriginal native community.'

This definition is applied in a number of statutes where the term 'African' is used without being defined. For example, in the Administration of Estates Act (Chapter 6:01) provision is made for the estate of an 'African'.[95] In the Customary Marriages Act (Chapter 5:07) there is reference to 'marriage between Africans'.[96]

- 'Law' means any enactment and the common law of Zimbabwe.
- 'Person' 'includes (a) any company incorporated or registered as such under an enactment; or (b) any body of persons, corporate or unincorporated; or (c) any local or other similar authority.
- 'Sign', with reference to a person who is unable to write his name, includes make his mark.

Definitions are followed by a set of substantive rules to apply to every enactment. Examples include the following:

- Words imparting the masculine gender include females and words in the singular include the plural and vice versa.[97]
- Where an enactment that has been amended is repealed such repeal shall repeal all enactments by which such first-mentioned enactment has been amended.
- Where an enactment repeals another enactment, the repeal shall not revive anything not in force or existing at the time at which the repeal takes effect.[98]
- A statutory instrument shall be published in the Gazette and shall come

into operation on the date of its publication unless some other date is fixed by or under the statutory instrument.[99]
- A reference in an enactment to a 'month' shall be construed as a reference to a 'calendar month' while a reference to a 'year' shall be construed as a reference to a period of twelve months.[100]
- Distance shall be measured in a straight line on a horizontal plane.[101]
- Where the time limited by an enactment for the doing of anything expires or falls upon a Saturday, a Sunday or a public holiday, the time so limited shall extend to, and the thing may be done on, the first following day that is not a Saturday, a Sunday or a public holiday.[102]

Interpretation of sections of a statute

Provisions in statutes defining terms usually take one of two forms: either that a particular word or expression 'means X' or that a particular word or expression 'includes X'. The use of the word 'means' signifies an exhaustive definition: anything else is excluded. In *Dilworth v Stamp Commissioner*, Lord Watson said:

> The word 'include' is very generally used in interpretation clauses in order to enlarge the meaning of words or phrases occurring in the body of the statute; and when it is so used these words or phrases must be construed as comprehending not only such things as they signify according to their natural import, but also those things, which the interpretation clause declares that they shall include.[103]

Preamble

Devenish describes a preamble as 'a recitation, usually couched in polished and eloquent phraseology, of the circumstances and reasons which have induced the legislature to enact the statute'.[104] Section 6 of the Interpretation Act says:

> The preamble to an enactment and any punctuation in an enactment shall form part of the enactment and may be used as aids to the construction of the enactment.

This provision merely declares a preamble to be part of an enactment and that it may be resorted to as an aid to interpretation, but does not say in what circumstances it may be employed as an aid. This position is to be determined by the courts. It would appear that the preamble may be used as an aid to interpretation, (i) where the words are ambiguous and (ii) in restricting wide language which goes beyond the purpose of the legislation. In the English case of *A.G. v Prince Ernest Augustus of Hanover*,

STATUTORY INTERPRETATION

Lord Normand said:

> When there is a preamble, it is generally in its recitals that the mischief to be remedied and the scope of the Act are described. It is therefore clearly permissible to have recourse to it as an aid to construing the enacting provisions. The preamble is not, however, of the same weight as an aid to construction of a Section of the Act as are other relevant enacting words to be found elsewhere in the Act or even in related Acts. There may be no exact correspondence between the preamble and the enactment, and the enactment may go beyond or it may fall short of the indications that may be gathered from the preamble. Again the preamble cannot be of much or any assistance in construing provisions which embody qualifications or exceptions from the operation of the general purpose of the Act. It is only when it conveys a clear and definite meaning in comparison with relatively obscure or indefinite enacting words that the preamble may legitimately prevail ... When the plaintiff puts forward one construction of an enactment and the defendant another, it is the court's business, in any case of some difficulty, after informing itself of what I have called the legal and factual context, including the preamble, to consider in the light of this knowledge whether the enacting words admit of both the rival constructions put forward. It they admit of only one construction, that construction will receive effect even if it is inconsistent with the preamble, but if the enacting words are capable of either of the constructions offered by the parties, the construction which fits the preamble may be preferred.[105]

The leading South African case is *Colonial Treasurer v Rand Water Board*, where Innes CJ said that the preamble is:

> [A] key to open the minds of the makers of the Act and the mischiefs which they intended to redress. But the key cannot be used if the meaning of the enacting clauses is clear and plain. In cases, however, where the wording is ambiguous, and in cases where the court is satisfied that the legislature must have intended to limit in some way the wide language used, then it is proper to have recourse to the preamble. It is often difficult to decide when the terms of an Act are so clear that they must be taken as they stand, and when it is permissible to call the aid of a preamble. The object must always be to ascertain the object of the legislature. And it may be necessary in arriving at such intention to cut down general language susceptible of restriction even though the words used are not ambiguous in themselves.[106]

One Zimbabwean case in which the issue of a preamble arose is *S v Davidson*.[107] In this case the appellant had been convicted by the Magistrates Court of contravening Section 36 of the Law and Order (Maintenance) Act (then Chapter 65) and sentenced to six months imprisonment with labour. Section 36 of the Law and Order (Maintenance) Act provided:

> Any person who in any public place or at any public meeting uses threatening,

abusive or insulting words or behaviour with intent to provoke a breach of the peace or whereby a breach of the peace is likely to be occasioned, shall be guilty of an offence ....

Under the definition section of the Act, Section 2 says:

[A] public place means any street, road, passage, square, park or recreation ground or any open space to which for the time being the public or any section thereof have or are permitted to have access, whether on payment or otherwise ....

The appellant was a lecturer at Belvedere Teachers Training College. His office in the adminstration block opened into the foyer of the building. On 20 October 1986, the lecturers of the college had gathered in the foyer of the administration block, having just heard of the untimely death of president Samora Machel in a plane crash in South Africa. They were discussing the circumstances of the plane crash and expressing their grief when the appellant opened the door of his office and came into the foyer and uttered words to the effect that the late president Samora Machel was on a Christmas shopping trip to Durban when his plane crashed. The appellant admitted uttering the words complained of, but contended that the words were not uttered in a 'public place' as defined by the Act. The magistrate had rejected this contention, holding that the preamble to the Act signified that the expression 'public place' had to be given an extended meaning for the 'maintenance of law and order in Zimbabwe'. The Supreme Court disagreed with the magistrate and emphasized that a preamble must only be resorted to where the enactment is unclear or ambiguous. In this case, the Supreme Court found the definition of 'public place' to be clear and unambiguous. Under the Act, a 'public place' denoted an 'open place'. Resorting to the preamble in order to make a foyer a ' public place' was held to be improper. The appellant's conviction was set aside.

The long title

The 'long title' is set out at the beginning of the Act and describes the general purposes of the Act. For example, the long title of the Interpretation Act says:

An Act to define certain terms when used in legislative enactments; to make provision with respect to the operation, commencement and interpretation of legislative enactments; to shorten the language of legislative enactments; and for other purposes.

The long title may be used as an aid to interpretation in exactly the same circumstances that regard may be had to a preamble. Thus, in *Bhyatt v Commissioner for Immigration* it was regarded as 'settled law' that 'in the process of ascertaining intention, it is permissible to have regard to the title of the Act'.[108]

The short title

This is the official name by which the statute is referred to. South African courts have said that regard may be had to it in the same way as with the long title to aid the process of interpretation.[109] Under English law, the short title is regarded as unhelpful and in a leading case it was said:

> [I]t is a statutory nickname to obviate the necessity of always referring to the Act under its full and descriptive title ... its object is identification and not description.[110]

The better approach is to have regard to the short title whenever it is useful in order to resolve ambiguities in statutory provisions.

Headings and marginal notes

The Interpretation Act appears to settle the place of headings and marginal notes. It provides in Section 7 as follows:

> In an enactment –
> (a) headings and marginal notes and other marginal references therein to other enactments; and
> (b) notes, tables, indexes and explanatory references inserted therein as part of any compilation or revision ... shall form no part of the enactment and shall be deemed to have been inserted for convenience of reference only.

This means that headings and marginal notes cannot be used as aids to statutory interpretation. The basis for this is that they 'form no part of the enactment'. This statutory position reflects the approach of English law on marginal notes.

In the leading English case of *Chandler v DPP*, Lord Reid had this to say:

> [S]ide notes cannot be used as an aid to construction. They are mere catchwords and I have never heard of it being supposed in recent times that an amendment to alter a side note could be proposed in either house of Parliament. Side notes in the original Bill are inserted by the draughtsman. So, side notes cannot be enacted in the same way as the long title or any part of the body of the Act.[111]

Punctuation

Section 6 of the Interpretation Act makes it clear that any form of punctuation in an enactment forms part of that enactment and may be used as an aid to interpretation. This settles a matter that has been unclear for some time in South African law. In *Bosman's Trustee v Land and Agricultural Bank of South Africa and Register of Deed Vryburg* punctuation was regarded as irrelevant in the interpretation of statutes.[112] The opposite view was preferred in *R v Njiwa*.[113] The Appellate Division left the question open in *Government of Lebowa v Government of the Republic of South Africa*.[114]

English law originally started on a note of disregarding punctuation but has now moved to use it as an aid to interpretation. In the English case of *Duke of Devonshire v O'Connor*, Lord Esher MR said:

> To my mind, however, it is perfectly clear that in an Act of Parliament there are no such things as brackets any more than there are such things as stops.[115]

This old view has been replaced by the one articulated by Lord Lowry in *Hanlon v Law Society* as follows:

> I consider that not to take account of punctuation disregards the reality that literate people, such as Parliamentary draughtsmen, punctuate what they write, if not identically, at least in accordance with grammatical principles. Why should not other literate people such as judges, look at the punctuations in order to interpret the meaning of the legislation as accepted by Parliament?[116]

Schedules

A schedule is found at the end of a statute. It is part of the statute and may be used as an aid to interpretation. The general rule is that where there is an irreconcilable conflict between a Schedule and a Section in the main body of the statute, the latter prevails.[117] In most cases, schedules contain specimen forms. In general, non-compliance with the exact form is not fatal, i.e, it will not invalidate what is done.[118]

External Aids

Historical background or surrounding circumstances

It is permissible to invoke the historical setting of a statute as an aid to the interpretation of ambiguous or unclear provisions. Circumstances that may be taken into account are those that the courts may take judicial notice of rather than where evidence of historical circumstances is required to be led. It may be said that the circumstances must be such that the court can say they are a matter of general knowledge.[119]

Parliamentary history, including parliamentary debates

Until 1993, English law firmly excluded parliamentary history as an aid to statutory interpretation. By 'parliamentary history' it is meant to cover both the pre-parliamentary materials such as reports of committees and commissions of enquiry and the parliamentary process itself (parliamentary debates, amendments in its passage in Parliament and proceedings in committees). In the case of *Miller v Taylor* the rule was stated and justified as follows:

> The sense and meaning of an Act of Parliament must be collected from what it says when passed into law: and not from the history of the changes it underwent in the house where it took its rise. That history is not known to the other house, or to the sovereign.[120]

Later cases were more explicit and emphatic. In *Fothergill v Monarch Airlines Ltd*, Diplock LJ said:

> The constitutional function performed by courts of justice as interpreters of the written law laid down in Acts of Parliament is often described as ascertaining 'the intention of Parliament' but what this metaphor, though convenient, omits to take into account is that the court, when acting in its interpretative role ... is doing so as mediator between the state in the exercise of its legislative power and the private citizen for whom the law made by Parliament constitutes a rule binding upon him and enforceable by the executive power of the state. Elementary justice ... demands that the rules by which the citizen is to be bound should be ascertainable by him (or more realistically by a competent lawyer advising him) by reference to identifiable sources that are publicly accessible. The source to which Parliament must have intended the citizen to refer is the language of the Act itself. These are the words that Parliament has itself approved as accurately expressing its intentions. If the meaning of those words is clear and unambiguous and does not lead to a result that is manifestly absurd or unreasonable, it would be a confidence trick by Parliament and destructive of all legal certainty if the private citizen could not rely upon that meaning but was required to search through all that had happened before and in the course of the legislative process in order to see whether there was anything to be found from which it could be inferred that Parliament's real intention had not been accurately expressed by the actual words that Parliament had adopted to communicate it to those affected by the legislation.[121]

Bennion lists nine reasons for the exclusionary rule:

1. It would be contrary to principle to allow reference to proceedings in Parliament.

2. What is said in one House is not known to the other House or to the Sovereign.
3. Allowing such reference would contravene the *parol* evidence rule.
4. Allowing such reference might contravene parliamentary privilege.
5. Allowing such reference would breach the comity that should exist between the courts and Parliament.
6. Allowing such reference would create difficulties for practitioners.
7. Allowing such reference would add to costs.
8. Parliamentary material is untrustworthy.
9. Allowing such reference would tend to undermine the reliability of the statute book.[122]

Several leading English cases have discussed the rule.[123] In 1992, in *Pepper v Hart*, the House of Lords demolished this rule by a majority decision and accepted the use of parliamentary history as an aid to interpretation.[124]

In Zimbabwe, the English rule has been followed with almost religious zeal. In the wake of *Pepper v Hart*, it was applied by the Zimbabwean Supreme Court and in *Tsvangirai v Registrar General* it accepted the use of parliamentary history as an aid to statutory interpretation. This position has now been sealed by Section 15B of the Interpretation Act, following an amendment made in 2002.[125]

Statutes *in pari materia*

Statutes are said to be *in pari materia* when they deal with identical subject matter. In other words, they may be said to be 'kindred legislation' dealing with the same subject matter.[126] The general rule appears to be that where an earlier statute is *in pari materia*, with a later one being considered by the court, any meanings attached to the earlier statute may be used as an aid in interpreting the later statute. The assumption for this approach is that the legislature intended uniformity in the meaning of the language.

In *Venter v Randburg Town Council* Nicholas J noted that if the same words appear in a subsequent Act *in pari materia*, 'the presumption arises that they are used in the meaning which has been judicially put upon them and that, unless there be something to rebut that presumption, the new statute is to be construed as the old one was'.[127]

In the Southern Rhodesian case of *National Industrial Credit Corp (Rhodesia) Ltd v Gumede and Another (2)* it was emphasized that for this *in pari materia* rule to apply, the previous judicial interpretation must be 'well settled and well recognized'.[128]

In cases where reliance is to be placed on a later statute *in pari materia* to interpret an earlier Act, it is only permissible where, either expressly or impliedly, it is clear that the legislature intended the later statute to explain the prior Act. Schereiner JA said the following:

> There is authority for the view that Acts of Parliament, without having been passed for the express purpose of explaining previous Acts, may nevertheless be used as 'legislative declarations' or 'Parliamentary expositions' of the meaning of such Acts .... It is, of course, the function of the courts to expound the true interpretation of the law ... but where Parliament has clearly shown in a later Act what is meant by an earlier one, it seems to me to be not only helpful but even proper to have regard to the later Act in interpreting the earlier.[129]

The *in pari materia* rule does not apply if a Zimbabwean statute is identical to *and* based on a foreign statute. This position was made clear by Young J in *Exparte Adair Properties Ltd*, where he said:

> [T]he fact that the wording of a statute follows that of a statute of another country does not mean that the interpretation given to a local statute will be the same as that given to similar wording in another country. One reason is that the context may differ. The duty of the court is to ascertain the meaning which the legislature of this country must be deemed to have intended. Nevertheless, decisions of the courts of another country on identically worded provisions are usually of high persuasive value.[130]

Treaties and International Conventions

A statute, or some of its provisions, may have been enacted in response to a treaty or other international convention. In terms of Section 111B of the Constitution of Zimbabwe, a treaty cannot have the effect of law unless incorporated by an Act of Parliament. Two situations are common here. The first is where an Act of Parliament expressly makes it law that a treaty shall be part of Zimbabwean law and puts the text of the treaty in a schedule. In such cases, there is little doubt that textbooks, expert opinion, judgments of foreign courts and *travaux preparatoires* of the treaty may be used as aids to the interpretation of the statute. The second situation is where the Act of Parliament implements the treaty without expressly incorporating its text. Here, the legislature chooses to use its own language. As long as the intention to implement the treaty is clear, such as where this appears in the preamble or long title, the courts will use the treaty as an aid, even if it is not expressly mentioned in the body of the statute. This is supported by English legal authority, for example, *Salomon v Commissioner of Customs and Excise*, where Diplock LJ said:

If from extrinsic evidence, it is plain that the enactment was intended to fulfill Her Majesty's Government's obligations under a particular convention, it matters not that there is no express reference to the convention in the statute. One must not presume that Parliament intends to break an international convention merely because it does not say expressly that it is intending to observe it.[131]

However it appears that the extent to which the treaty is used as an aid in this situation is limited: the treaty is only considered where the words of the statute are ambiguous or unclear. This was emphasized by Diplock LJ as follows:

> If the terms of the legislation are clear and unambiguous, they must be given effect to, whether or not they carry out Her Majesty's treaty obligations, for the sovereign power of the Queen in Parliament extends to breaking treaties ... any remedy for such a breach of an international obligation lies in a forum other than Her Majesty's own courts.[132]

This statement was supported by the concurring speeches of Lords Bridge and Oliver. Lord Oliver said:

> It can only apply where the expression of the legislative intention is genuinely ambiguous or obscure or where a literal or prima facie construction leads to a manifest absurdity and where the difficulty can be resolved by a clear statement directed to the matter in issue.[133]

Lord Bridge indicated that resort to *Hansard* should only be made 'in the rare cases where the very issue of interpretation that the courts are called on to resolve has been addressed in parliamentary debate and where the promoter of the legislation has made a clear statement directed to that very issue'.[134]

Notes

1. *Canadian Bar Review*, 1938 (16) 1, p. 16.
2. See F.A.R. Bennion (2002) *Statutory Interpretation*, Fourth edition. London: LexisNexisButterworths, pp. 3-4.
3. See *R v Judge of City of London Court* 1892 (1) QB27.
4. See *Venter v R* 1907 TS 190.
5. 1951 (4) SA 400 (AD), p. 410.
6. 1998 (1) ZLR 188 (H).
7. For examples of references to dictionaries in South Africa, see *Minister of the Interior v Machadorp Investments* (1957 (2) SA 395 (AD), p. 402, and *Slabbert v Minister van Lande* (1963 (3) SA 620 (T), p. 621.
8. 2000 (2) ZRL 469(S).

9. See *State v Collop* 1981 (1) SA 150 (AD), p. 161.
10. See *R v Padsha* 1923 AD 281, p. 295; *Moller v Kiemoes School Committee*, 1911 AD 635.
11. 1970 (4) SA1 (RAD), p. 4.
12. 1962 (1) SA 458 (AD), p. 476.
13. 1957 AC 436, p. 461.
14. 1977 (1) SA 665 (AD).
15. SC 47/04.
16. 1963 (1) Ch. 1 (CA).
17. See *River Wear Commissioners v Adamson* (1877) 2 AC 743, p. 764.
18. 1965 *RLR* 162.
19. See also *S v Masiriva* 1990 ZLR 373.
20. 1990 (2) ZLR 373(HC).
21. See page 387F.
22. See *Black-Clawson International* (1975) AC 591.
23. See Rupert Cross, John Bell and Sir George Engle (1987) *Statutory Interpretation*, London: Butterworths, p. 11.
24. See Bennion (2002), p. 344, paragraph 142.
25. 1979 (2) SA 255 (R).
26. Ibid. p. 257.
27. 1973 (2) SA 14 (RAD), p. 26.
28. D.E. Devenish (1992) *Interpretation of Statutes*. First edition, Cape Town: Juta & Co., p. 77.
29. 1964 (2) QB7; (1964) 1 ALL Employment Regulations 628.
30. See Cross et al. (1987), p. 1132.
31. See G. Cockram (1987) *The Interpretation of Statutes*. Third edition. Cape Town: Juta and Co., p. 153.
32. 1980 AC 744, pp. 807-8.
33. The Sunday Observance Act (1677).
34. 1931 TPD 443.
35. See *S v Makandigona* 1981 (4) SA 439 (ZAD).
36. See *Quazi v Quazi* (1980) AC 744.
37. See *S v Makandigona* 1981 (4) SA 439 (ZAD).
38. 1986 (2) ZLR 269 (SC).
39. Gubbay JA, p. 277.
40. 1977 AC 699; 1976 (3) ALL ER 775.
41. See *Amberley Estates (Pvt.) Ltd v Controller of Customs and Excise* 1986 (2) ZLR 269 (SC), p. 277.
42. 1977 (2) SA 774 (T).
43. 1967 (1) WLR 691, p. 578.
44. 1968 (1) QB 479.
45. Quoted in Cross et al. (1987), p. 137.
46. (1953) IWLR 974.

47. (1831) 2B & Ad 592.
48. Bennion (2002), p. 844.
49. 1762 (3) Burr 1341.
50. 1984 (2) All ER 495
51. Cross (1987) pp. 138-9.
52. 1969 (4) SA 179 (RAD).
53. See Cross et al. (1987), p. 145.
54. See *Randfontein Estates Gold Mining Co v Minister of Finance* 1928 WLD 83.
55. 1981 AC 124, pp. 193-4.
56. Bennion (2002), paragraph 387, p. 842.
57. See Devenish (1992), p. 75.
58. Bennion (2002), pp. 387, 842.
59. 1851 (16) QB 496.
60. Quoted in Devenish (1992), p. 67, n96.
61. 1981 (3) SA 800 (ZB).
62. Ibid., p.803 A-D.
63. See Cross et al. (1987), p. 167.
64. See D.V. Cowen (1980) 'The Interpretation of Statutes and the Concept of the Intention of the Legislature', in *Tydskrif vir Hedendaagse Romeins-Hollandse Reg (THRHR)* 43 (*Journal of Contemporary Dutch Law*) 374, p. 392.
65. 1981 QB 758; 1981 (1) ALL ER 769.
66. 1981 Q.B. 767. See also *Re Sigsworth* 1935, Chapter 89.
67. 1973 (2) SA 14 (RA).
68. 1975 AC 591, p. 614.
69. [1912] AC 305.
70. 1996 (1) *ZLR* 664(S).
71. See Bennion (2002), para 128.
72. 1931 AD 323, pp. 336-7.
73. 1953 (1) SA 392 (A), 399H.
74. per De Villiers JA in *Commissioner for Inland Revenue v George Forest Timber Co Ltd.* 1924 AD 51, pp. 531-2.
75. [1982] AC 300, p. 323.
76. 1887 (19) QBD 629, p. 638.
77. 1983 (2) *ZLR* 376.
78. Ibid., pp. 382A-383A.
79. Ibid., p. 383D.
80. 1988 (2) *ZLR* 27 (HC).
81. SC 20/03.
82. 1911 AD 1, p. 8.
83. 1928 AD 435, p. 450.
84. 1995 (1) *ZLR* 80 (5), p. 84 G-H.
85. See pp. 338H-339A.
86. See pp. 428H-429B.

87. See Devenish (1992), p. 178.
88. 1994 (2) *ZLR* 329 (S).
89. 1990 (2) *ZLR* 48 (HC).
90. See p. 63C-G.
91. 1928 AD 286, p. 290.
92. See *Ex parte Adair Properties (Pvt.) Ltd* 1967 (2) SA 622 (R), p. 627.
93. See Section 2 (2).
94. See G.C. Thornton (1987) *Legislative Drafting*. Third edition. London: Butterworths Law, p. 100.
95. See Section 68.
96. See Section 12.
97. Section 9.
98. Section 17 (1) (a).
99. Section 20 (1).
100. Section 33 (96).
101. Section 34.
102. Section 33 (4).
103. 1899 AC 99, pp. 105-6.
104. See p. 102.
105. 1957 AC 436, p. 467.
106. 1907 TS 479, p. 482.
107. 1988 (3) SA 252 (ZS).
108. 1932 AD 125, p. 129.
109. See *R v Sisulu & Others* 1953 (3) SA 276 (A), p. 287.
110. See *Vacher & Sons Ltd v London Society of Compositors* 1913 AC 107, pp. 128-9.
111. 1964 AC 763, p. 789.
112. 1916 CPD 47.
113. 1957 (2) SA 5 (N).
114. 1988 (1) SA 344 (A).
115. 1890 (24) QBD 468, p. 478.
116. 1981 AC 124, p. 198.
117. See *African and European Investment Co. Ltd v Warren & Others* 1924 AD 308, p. 360.
118. See *Liquidators Wapejo Shipping Company Ltd v Lurie Bros* 1924 AD 69, p. 72. See also Section 5 (1) of the Interpretation Act, which says where a form is prescribed or specified by any enactment, deviations therefrom not materially affecting the substance nor calculated to mislead shall not invalidate the form used.
119. See *Hleka v Johannesburg City Council* 1949 (1) SA 842 (A); *Chandler v Director of Public Prosecutions* 1964 AC 763.
120. 1769 (4) Burr, pp. 2303, 2332.
121. 1981 AC 251, pp. 279-80.

122. See Bennion (2002), p. 546.
123. See, for example, *Black-Clawson International Ltd v Papierwerke Waldhof-Aschaffenburg Attorney General* 1975 AC 591.
124. 1993 All Employment Regulations 42.
125. The Amendments were effected through the General Laws Amendment (No. 2) (Act No. 14 of 2002), Section 2.
126. See Devenish (1992), p. 133.
127. 302 (w), p. 306.
128. 1964 (4) SA 258 (SR), p. 261.
129. *Patel v Minister of the Interior and Another* 1955 (2) SA 485 (A), p. 493.
130. 1967 (2) SA 622, pp. 623-4.
131. 1967 (2) QB 116, p. 144.
132. Ibid., p. 143. See also *Quazi v Quazi* 1980 AC 744, p. 808.
133. 1967 (2) QB 116, p. 52.
134. Ibid., p. 49.

Some Latin Words & Expressions

A fuller list of Latin expressions and maxims is contained in *An Introduction to Law* (1983).[1] Reference must also be made to *Black's Law Dictionary*.[2]

a fortiori – for the stronger reason
a temporae morae – from the time of default
ab extra – extra; beyond
ab initio – from the beginning
ab intestato – by intestacy
ab irato – by one who is angry
ad idem – of the same mind or in agreement
ad infinitum – to an indefinite extent
ad libitum – at pleasure
alibi – elsewhere, i.e., a defence in criminal law which relies on the fact of having been elsewhere when an offence was committed
allocutus – a formal and authoritative speech; an address.
amicus curiae – a friend of the court
animus contrahendi – the intention to contract
animus furandi – the intention of stealing
animus injuriandi – the intention of injury
ante omnia – before anything else is done
arguendo – for the sake of argument
audi alteram partem – hear the other side
autrefois acquit – formerly acquitted

SOME LATIN WORDS & EXPRESSIONS

autrefois convict – formerly convicted
bona fide – in good faith
brutum fulmen – something ineffectual. Usually applied to a judgment that is, in legal effect, no judgment at all.
cadit quaestio – the question falls to the ground; the dispute is over
caeteris paribus – other things being equal
capax doli – capable of wrongdoing
casus belli – an act or circumstance that provokes or justifies war
casus fortuitus – unavoidable accident
casus major – an extraordinary casualty
casus omissus – an omitted contingency. This mainly refers to a situation not provided for by a statute or contract
causa causans – the immediate cause
causa sine qua non – the cause without which the thing cannot be or the event would not have occurred.
caveat emptor – let the purchaser beware
caveat venditor – let the seller beware
cessante ratione legis, cessat ipsa lex – the reason of the law ceasing, the law itself ceases
cesset executio – literally, 'let execution stay'. This refers to an order directing a delay in execution
compos mentis – master of one's mind; of sound mind
confession in judicio – confession in court
consensus ad idem – a meeting of minds
contemporanea expositio – contemporaneous exposition
contra bonos mores – contrary to public morality
corpus delicti – the body, substance or foundation of an alleged crime
court a quo – a court from which a case has been appealed
culpa – fault
curator ad litem – curator for the purpose of litigation
curator bonis – a guardian of property
curia advisari vult – the court desires to consider its judgment
de bonis propriis – of his own goods
de facto – according to the fact
de jure – according to the law
delegata potestas non potest delegari – a delegated power cannot be delegated
de minimis non curat lex – the law does not concern itself with trivialities
de novo – afresh

SOME LATIN WORDS & EXPRESSIONS

dies induciae – days of grace allowed
dolus – fraud, intent
domicilium citandi – domicile for the purpose of service court process
dominium – ownership
e contra – on the contrary
e converso – conversely, on the other hand
eo nomine – by that name
ejusdem generis – of the same kind
ex cathedra – literally, 'from the chair', i.e., from the seat of authority
ex curia – out of court
et al – and other persons (et al.)
et seq – and the following one(s)
exempli gratia – by way of example
ex abundanti cautela – out of abundant caution
ex facie – on the face of it
ex gratia – as a favour; not legally necessary.
ex hypothesi – hypothetically
ex legibus – according to the laws
ex mandato – according to the mandate
ex mero motu – from one's own intitiative
ex officio – by virtue of office
ex parte – from one side
ex post facto – after the event
expressio unius personae vel rei, est exclusio alterius – the express mention of one person or thing is the exclusion of another.
ex tempore – on the spur of the moment, not premeditated
ex turpi causa non oritur actio – an action does not arise from an immoral or base cause
ex visceribus verborum – from the mere words (and nothing else)
falsus in uno, falsus in omnibus – false is one, false in all
flagrante delicto – in the act of committing a crime
furtum usus – theft of the use of a thing
generalia specialibus non derogant – universal things do not detract from specific things
habeas corpus – literally, 'to have the body'. It refers to a writ requiring a person to be brought to court in order that the lawfulness of his detention be investigated.
ibid. (ibidem) – in the same place. It is used in citations to refer to the work

SOME LATIN WORDS & EXPRESSIONS

cited immediately before and that the cited matter appears on the same page of the same book (unless a different page is specified)
id est – that is (i.e.)
ideo consideratum est – therefore it is considered
ignoratia, facti excusat – ignorance of fact is an excuse
ignoratia juris neminem excusat – ignorance of the law excuses no one
in camera – in chambers or in private
in forma pauperis – in the manner of a pauper
in jure non remota causa, sed proxima spectatur – in law the proximate, and not the remote cause is to be regarded
in limine – at the outset
in loco parentis – in the place of a parent
in pari delicto, potior est conditio possidentis (or *defendentis*) – in equal fault, the condition of the possessor (or defendant) is the best.
in pari materia – relating to the same matter
in re – in the matter of
inter alia – among other things
in toto – altogether
intra vires – within the power
ipse dixit – 'he himself said it', applied where something is asserted without being proved
ipsissima verba – the identical/exact words used by somebody being quoted
ipso facto – by the mere fact
ipso jure – by the law itself
justitia – justice
lex non cogit ad impossibilia – the law does not compel the impossible
locus classicas – a classical passage from an acknowledged authority
locus standi – place of standing. This refers to the right to bring an action or to defend an action or to be heard in a given forum.
mala fide – in bad faith
mens rea – criminal intention
merx – trade articles, merchandise
modus operandi – a manner of operating
mutatis mutandis – with the necessary changes
necessitas non habet legem – necessity has no law
nec vi, nec clam, nec precario – neither by force, nor by stealth, nor by request
nemo data qui non habet – no one gives who possesses not
nemo debet esse judex in propria causa – no one should be judge in his own

SOME LATIN WORDS & EXPRESSIONS

cause
nemo tenetur se ipsum accusare – no one is bound to criminate himself
nisi – unless
nolle prosequi – unwilling to prosecute
noscitur a sociis – a thing is known by its associates
nulla bona – no goods
nulla poena sine culpa – no punishment without fault
obiter dictum – said incidentally
omne quod solo inaedificatur solo cedit – everything which is built upon the soil passes with the soil
onus probandi – the burden of proof
particeps criminis – an accessory to a crime
prima facie – on the face of it, at first sight
pro bono publico – for the public good
pro deo – literally, 'for God'. Used to refer to a lawyer appointed by the court to represent a pauper without legal fees
pro forma – as a matter of form
pro privato comodo – for private convenience
pro rata – for a proportion
quid pro quo – something for something
qui facit per alium facit per se – he/she who does anything by another does it by him/herself
quod erat demonstratum (QED) – that which has been proved
ratio decidendi – reason for the decision
reddendo singula singulis – arranging or applying each to each
res – a thing
res ipsa loquitur – the thing speaks for itself
res judicata – the thing has been decided
restitutio in integrum – restitution or restoration in full
simul et semel – at one and the same time
sine die – without a day fixed
socius criminis – an accomplice in the commission of a crime
solatium – comfort
spes – hope or expectation
spoliatus ante omnia restituendus est – the despoiled ought to be restored before anything else
stare decisis – to stand by the decision
stare decisis et non quieta movere – to stand by the decision and not to dis-

turb settled points
status quo – the position as it was before
subsecuta observatio – the usage of a word over a long period of time
sui generis – of its own class
uberrima fides – the utmost good faith
ubi jus ibi remedium – where there is a right, there is a remedy
ultra vires – beyond the power
ut res magis valeat quam pereat – it is better for a thing to have effect than to be made void
versari in re illicita – liability for the consequences following an unlawful act
vis major – irresistible force
viva voce – orally, by the living voice
volenti non fit injuria – that to which a man consents cannot be regarded as an injury

Notes

1. D.A. Reynolds and J.A. Russel (1983) *An Introduction to Law.* Government of Zimbabwe: Ministry of Justice.
2. Bryon A. Garner (ed.) (2004) *Black's Law Dictionary.* Eighth edition. Eagen, MS: Thomson West.

NOTES

NOTES

NOTES

NOTES